PREFABULOUS
+SUSTAINABLE

SHERI KOONES

FOREWORD BY ROBERT REDFORD

PREFABULOUS
+SUSTAINABLE

BUILDING AND CUSTOMIZING AN AFFORDABLE, ENERGY-EFFICIENT HOME

Abrams, New York

For my brother, Mark Warman
And sister, Barbara Corpuel
With love.

ACKNOWLEDGMENTS

All my books have been inspired by a desire to share information and new ways to build with other homeowners. But this book has been inspired by a far greater cause. It is becoming clear that we must all change our mode of transportation and the way we build our homes, one of the biggest strains on materials and energy. We need to consider using more efficient cars and even bicycles whenever possible. If we hope to leave our children with a planet that can supply them with all their needs, we need to consider how we are using our resources today—particularly in building our houses.

Having spent the last several years researching prefabricated construction and green alternatives, I have wondered over these years why it has taken so long to make the transition to using these options. There are so many systems and materials available to make it easier to build an eco-friendly house. With this increase in options, the prices are also beginning to make these materials more accessible to everyone building a home.

I have been so inspired by all the green conferences I've attended and participated in, that have worked so hard to make available valuable information to building professionals. They are very worthwhile endeavors, and I'm so appreciative of their efforts.

I'd like to thank all my friends who are constantly encouraging me to forge ahead. My dear friend Dr. Isabel Leeds reminds me every Thursday morning that I must move ahead with these efforts, even when they are grueling. Thanks to Lucy Hedrick and Denise Marcil for your help and support. My professional friends, Dave Wrocklage, Steve Bassett, John Colucci, and Jerry and Scott Rouleau, are forever sharing their knowledge and encouragement.

A special thank you to all the homeowners, architects, builders, photographers, and suppliers who took the time to share their experiences and expertise with me. Also to faculty adviser Amy E. Gardner at the University of Maryland, who was such a joy to work with. Thank you to Robert Redford for his generous contribution to this book and to Joyce Deep for your kindness and help through this process.

Jeremy Bertrand of the Building Systems Council has continuously encouraged my projects and graciously helped in so many ways to bring these last several books to fruition—I'm very grateful for all your efforts.

A big thank you to my editor, Rebecca Kaplan, and designer, Darilyn Lowe Carnes, for their fine work.

My very special thanks to Steve Culpepper, who made this project happen.

And I am so grateful to my family, Rob, Alex, and Jess, who continue to inspire me and whose love propels me to want to write the best book possible and to help make it a better world for them.

—Sheri Koones

Most of the plantings around the house are native to the area, such as the red maples, cedars, oak, black-eyed Susans, and cornflowers. Native plants withstand the harsh weather and require minimal care. The trellis on both sides of the rear of the house offers some shading for sitting areas.

CONTENTS

Over the years it has been my mission to protect the environment—our oceans, forests, and the pristine beauty of this country that is our legacy. My concern has always been that if we destroy this land that has been here for billions of years for short-term gain, it can never be replaced. We need to preserve this land so we have something valuable to hand down to our children and our children's children.

For many years we have been dependent on nonrenewable energy sources such as coal, oil, and gas. This has made us dependent on foreign oil and has created a fear that has motivated some to want to rip apart our cherished land to make us more fuel independent. Instead of looking for more nonrenewable fuel, we should all be considering the advantages of using renewable energy sources, such as solar, geothermal, and wind, that are totally viable, safe, clean, and economically superior. New technologies are developed each year that can harness this energy, reducing our need for fuel, and creating more healthy environments. Products are becoming available that have reduced embodied energy and are made from recycled materials that have in the past ended up in our landfills.

In the last thirty years we have been successful at passing laws to protect the environment. The National Environmental Policy Act (NEPA), for one, requires federal agencies to integrate environmental values into their decision-making processes by considering the environmental impacts of their proposed actions and reasonable alternatives to those actions. As individuals, we can decrease the need for fossil fuels in our own lives. Since homes represent approximately 20 percent of the United States' energy use, decreasing energy in the home will reduce the need for fossil fuel and preserve our resources while also saving homeowners money in fuel costs.

Prefabulous and Sustainable offers many wonderful examples of houses that have been built requiring minimum energy from nonrenewable sources. Passive solar techniques were employed to limit the need for excess energy, and in some cases, solar and geothermal energy techniques supplemented energy needs. All the houses employed methods of preventing energy loss through various means, such as using superior insulation, limiting waste through prefab methods, creating healthy environments using less toxic products, and utilizing recycled products, which helps limit what goes into our landfills. The houses in this book show that beautiful houses can be built that will be kinder and gentler to the environment and reduce water consumption and energy.

The defense of our environment is crucial and it is important that it be preserved for future generations. *Prefabulous and Sustainable* will inspire you to consider more environmentally friendly options and show you how to create homes that will bring balance to our future.

—Robert Redford

Environmentalist, Actor, Director

OPPOSITE The Tucker Bayou House in WaterSound, Florida. (Photo by Jack Gurdnel)

9

INTRODUCTION

Over the years, as the author of several books on home construction, I've explored many of the ways that people build. Nothing, though, impresses me more than the amazing evolution of prefabrication. Think of the Sears kit houses at the turn of the last century—quality homes that arrived on trucks in precut parts and were erected by a local builder. Prefab houses have been around for years. Yet most people think of prefab as a term for mobile homes and poor-quality construction. While this was true for a period of time after the Second World War, today's prefabricated homes are state of the art. They are energy efficient and come in virtually any style of architecture and countless sizes. Prefabs can be high-end or fit a tight budget.

Prefab offers speedy construction and tight, energy-efficient quality. Raising a new prefab house brings much less traffic and disturbance to the neighborhood than conventional construction. Prefab can also mean lower costs and faster mortgages.

I've been wowed by the beauty prefab architects, manufacturers, and builders achieve. I've visited factories all around the country, and I'm repeatedly impressed with the accuracy and technology that goes into their production. But the single most impressive aspect of prefab construction is its ecological, or "green," advantage. If you visit a factory, you will see firsthand the resource conservation that is at the core of prefab construction. Factories employ the latest energy-efficient technology and use nontoxic products to create healthy home environments. Energy and resource conservation have become more than issues of personal choice; they are *the* global concern of our day.

For years I'd heard about global warming without a clear understanding of its significance. It appeared to be such a huge problem that nothing one person could do would ever possibly matter. Now, however, it's clear to me that only individuals can make a difference. Acting as a community of concerned individuals, we can turn things around. Whether it's driving less, making do with what we have, repairing something rather than replacing it, or even changing out old incandescent bulbs for compact fluorescent ones—the impact of our decisions and actions grows.

Nothing in our lives costs more than our houses. So when we build, we need to ask the following: What kind of roofing, siding, flooring, paint, construction method, foundation, insulation, windows and doors, cabinets, systems, and fixtures should we use? It all adds up. Building green or sustainable houses can make a huge environmental difference.

WHY WE NEED GREEN HOUSES

One of the goals participants of the 1997 Kyoto Protocol put forth was to reduce carbon output by cutting household emissions by 1,500 pounds per person per year. According to Carbonfund.org, every one of us in this country is

OPPOSITE The Henry Allerton Lakehouse in Colchester, Vermont, was designed and manufactured by Connor Homes and built by Laberge Building Company. This beautiful panelized house received a LEED-H certification, ENERGY STAR rating and a Vermont Residential Building Energy Standards (REBS) Certificate. (Photo by Connor Homes)

responsible for an annual carbon dioxide output of 50,715 pounds. Replace your old washer with an ENERGY STAR model and reduce your output by 500 pounds; lower the temperature of your hot water heater by 10 degrees and reduce your output by 600 pounds; replace old bulbs with energy-efficient ones and reduce your output by another 100 pounds or more.

For even more dramatic reductions in your personal carbon output, make sure your next house is as energy efficient as you can make it. This will reduce the energy needed to heat and cool your home, thereby reducing your utility bills and, ultimately, your carbon footprint.

PREFAB IS INTRINSICALLY GREEN

One of the best individual responses to these pressing environmental issues is prefabricated construction. Every type of prefab starts in a controlled environment protected from the rain, snow, and vast changes in temperature that can cause materials to twist, swell, warp, and mildew. Building lumber that is crooked and twisted joins together poorly, leaving gaps that can lead to heat loss in winter and heat gain in summer. Moreover, wet framing studs become fertile ground for mildew, which seriously diminishes the quality of indoor air. Opting for prefab allows you to sidestep these issues. Doing so also substantially reduces waste. Construction of the average 2,000 square-foot house generates 4 tons of waste. You pay for everything that goes into your house, including what's thrown away. On top of that, you pay for the dumpster that holds the waste, you pay for it to be hauled away, and you pay the "tipping" charges at the dump when the waste arrives. Saving time and material saves money. And every builder today wants to save money.

Many manufacturers, architects, and build-

BELOW Panels are produced in the factory under controlled conditions, with waste kept to a minimum. (Photo by Connor Homes)

BOTTOM Cutoffs can be seen at this panel company, neatly stacked and labeled so they can be reused. (Photo by Connor Homes)

ers are able to meet the increasing demand for greener construction by using prefabrication. However, prefab isn't just a way of building—it's many different ways of building. The following are some of the most common methods.

Modular

Modular houses are composed of one or more *modules,* or boxes, which people assemble in factories, transport by truck, and join together on a pre-poured foundation. As with each house in this book, modular houses are built to comply with the local building codes. They often arrive in various states of completeness upon delivery, but however finished the modules are when delivered, all are quickly closed up and made weather-tight (something that's impossible with site-built construction). Morever, you can construct modular houses in as little as a week.

By employing modular construction, much of the waste generated by traditional houses is avoided. Wood that would ordinarily be wasted is recycled for other uses: It can be burned for heating, or the smaller pieces—which may be thrown in the dumpster on a job site—are combined to form engineered lumber used in other projects.

Many factories return leftover drywall to the manufacturer to be recycled. And because workers live near the factories, they travel much less than they would if they were going to a series of different job sites. Also, contractors such as plumbers and electricians can work on several houses in a day at the same facility so they are not expending gas going to a variety of house construction sites to do their work.

Structural Insulated Panels

Structural Insulated Panels (SIPs) are panels that are manufactured by sandwiching foam insulation between two outer, structural panels of wood (usually oriented strand board or plywood). Other materials, such as metal can also be used for the outer shells. SIPs form a strong and continuous barrier against the elements because each panel mates tightly with the next. Factories often send panels out with openings cut for doors and windows, though sometimes they cut them out on site.

Tests show SIPs to be very energy efficient and to substantially cut down on heating and cooling costs. They are also easier and faster to erect than traditional site-built houses.

Panelized Construction

Panels can be constructed with SIPs, or by using standard frame construction, though in both cases they are built in an enclosed environment. In standard wood-frame panelization, factories build transportable sections of a house in the factory in much the same way as those built on-site. Then they send finished panels on trucks to the site, and workers install them, much the way you assemble a jigsaw puzzle. Windows and doors often are preinstalled. As with modular construction, panel factories reuse much of the material for other projects, which substantially

BELOW Michelle Kaufmann teamed up with All American Homes, a manufacturer of modular houses, to build a house which was on display at the Chicago's Museum of Science and Industry as part of the Small Home: Green and Wired exhibition. The design, innovative materials and systems together created an environmentally healthy house that is also very energy efficient. (mkSolaire Smart Home by Michelle Kaufmann/photos courtesy of John Swain)

BELOW The DESIGNhabitat 2 House integrates design quality and energy efficiency using the modular process. A team of architecture students and faculty (David Hinson and Stacy Norman) from The School of Architecture, Auburn University partnered with a modular company, Palm Harbor Homes to design and build a modular Habitat for Humanity home for a family displaced by Hurricane Katrina. (Photograph by Stacy Norman)

BOTTOM One of the units in transit to the home site. (Photograph by David Hinson)

reduces waste. In a 1996 study*, a panelized house and a traditionally built house were erected side by side. The panelized construction saved 253 man hours, 5,300 feet of lumber, produced 13 less cubic yards of waste, and less in cleanup costs, in addition to a 16 percent savings in the cost of framing. Panelization conserves lumber and construction time, and reduces cleanup costs and waste.

Timber Frame

Think of timber frames as really big furniture. Just as beautiful furniture is crafted and put together, so are timber frames built as well. One of the oldest ways of building in this country, Asia, and Europe, timber frames are self-supporting structures that workers connect with mortise-and-tenon joints (joints formed by inserting the end of one piece of timber into a hole cut in the other). Post-and-beam construction (when wall posts directly support roof and floor beams) is similar, except connections are often made with metal, where as timber frames are built out of solid timbers. Post-and-beam construction, may also include engineered wood, such as glulams, Parallel Strand Lumber (PSL), or Laminated Veneer Lumber (LVL). Many of today's timber framers use standing dead wood, river wood, reclaimed wood, and wood that has been purchased from managed forests. When a timber frame is taken apart, the wood can be used to build something else. Timber framers often purchase lumber from local suppliers, which cuts down on transportation costs. Oftentimes, the walls that envelop many timber frame houses are made with SIPs or panels, further limiting the amount of waste generated and man-hours necessary for construction.

*Framing the American Dream by the Structural Building Components Association (formerly WTCA). www.sbcindustry.com/fad.php.

BELOW The Hammond Residence, in St. Paul, Minnesota, received a five star ENERGY STAR rating. Energy efficiency is achieved with passive solar design, triple-pane low-E windows, high efficiency radiant heating, geothermal heating, ENERGY STAR appliances, fluorescent lighting, insulated concrete foundation walls, and structural insulated panels. The house includes recycled materials, such as solid surface countertops; healthy interior elements, such as low-VOC adhesives and water conservation measures, such as low-flow faucets and a rainwater capture system. The structural insulated panels were produced by Extreme Panel Technologies, the house was designed by Michael Huber Architects and built by Panelworks Plus, Inc. (Photo by homeowner)

BELOW A SIPs panel lifted into place for the Hammond House. (Photo by homeowner)

BOTTOM The panels go up quickly, limiting their exposure to the elements. (Photo by homeowner)

Steel Frame

Commercial construction has long depended on prefabricated steel frames. Using steel for residential construction however is a fairly recent development. People choose steel because it is durable, resistant to fire, mold, rot, and insect damage, and is strong enough to span large distances without support. You can use heavy gauge red iron to create a timber-frame type structure, or substitute light-gauge steel studs for wood, similar to the way wood-frame houses are built. Steel is being used to creatively build strong, durable homes. Metal is also one of the most recyclable materials in the world. Most of the metal we use for construction has been recycled, and can be recycled again. In addition, it is one of the strongest building materials out there, so if you construct a home with steel, you can expect it to stand for a very long time.

ADDITIONAL GREEN MEASURES

Besides all the intrinsically green qualities of prefab construction, many individuals are taking additional measures to improve prefab's green quotient. These are just a few of the materials, strategies, and systems being implemented right now to make a difference:

• Passive solar design. Refers to positioning a house and placing its windows in a way that takes fullest advantage of sunlight and the sun's warmth.

• Active solar design. Involves installing photovoltaic roof panels to convert the sun's rays into electricity or solar hot water panels to heat water for domestic and heating uses.

• High-efficiency systems for heating and cooling (geothermal system), irrigation (rainwater collection systems), hot water (efficient and on-demand units), and wind power (using wind turbines).

- Recycled or reclaimed timbers and other sustainable materials for construction.
- Energy-efficient fixtures and controls. Lighting that takes advantage of daylight to reduce the need for electricity and more efficient bulbs. In addition, sensors and timers can turn off lights when they're not in use.
- Strategies that ensure the durability of the house and its adaptability over time.
- High-efficiency insulation and windows. These increase the energy efficiency of the house, make it more comfortable, and reduce utility costs.
- Interior furnishings that minimize chemical emissions and promote good air quality.
- Energy-efficient appliances that carry an ENERGY STAR rating.
- Building in areas that are close to schools, work, recreation, and public transportation to limit the need to travel by car.
- Selecting drought-tolerant native plants to limit the need for irrigation.

DEFINING AND MEASURING GREEN

Because of the relatively recent and significant emphasis on green construction, the need arose to better define and measure *greenness*. People have developed various rating systems, such as the voluntary guidelines set forth by the National Association of Home Builders and their new certification program, the National Green Building Standard. But currently the most widely used and respected voluntary rating system is the Leadership in Energy and Environmental Design (LEED), created by the United States Green Building Council (USGBC).

LEED helps define sustainable design by using a 4-level certification program (based on a points system). LEED Certified homes need a minimum of 40 points; LEED Silver need a minimum of 50 points; LEED Gold need a minimum of 60 points; and LEED Platinum need a minimum of 80 points.

The NAHB system similarly works on a 4 level point system. People also use numerous local rating systems to define and rate home construction as well. These ratings give architects a framework within which to design energy-efficient houses using sustainable materials, and systems and solar orientation. Ratings also help homeowners understand the level of sustainability they can expect from their house.

PREFABULOUS AND SUSTAINABLE: THE BOOK

In case you can't tell, when it comes to prefab, I'm a believer. I'm convinced that prefab is the most efficient and healthy method of building a house.

Just as we've become accustomed to advanced technology and constant improvements in all the other products we purchase—cars, computers, appliances—we should request the same efficiency in our homes. In fact, I'm convinced that within a decade or two we will be building nearly every house, either partly or wholly using prefabrication. Current methods of prefab, plus the inevitable refinements that science and technology will bring, promise a bright future for the home-construction industry and for our homes.

Homeowners are rightfully hungry for energy-efficient, healthy homes that will stand up to weather and time. When additional energy-efficient methods and materials are used in conjunction with prefabrication, a myriad of solutions take shape. The result is houses that will endure.

The homes in this book illustrate the many types of prefab construction and combinations of prefab methods. In the book, I describe the green aspects of each structure, as well as rate their level of "greenness" (*green*, *greener*, or *greenest*). All the houses included in this book are quite

The Topel Residence was designed by architect Matthew Moger and built in Pennsylvania by Hugh Loftig Timber Framing, using prefabricated structural insulated panels and incorporating a timber frame for the common areas of the house. The house received LEED for Homes Gold certification. (Photo courtesy of John M. Lewis Photo)

green, so the divisions may seem blurry. However, this last group, the *greenest*, includes remarkable houses that have mostly achieved national certification, ENERGY STAR ratings and use a minimum of energy.

The twenty-five prefab houses profiled in this book are a testament to the beauty, sustainability, and healthy environments that you can achieve using green construction. Some of these houses are the very greenest in North America. The houses vary in style, design, type of construction, and size, but all are prefabricated, and all have a level of sustainability beyond the inherent qualities of prefab.

1

GREEN HOUSES

"It's not easy being green," the great green original once famously lamented. Back in 1969, when Kermit the Frog made his debut, he was probably right. But today, being green couldn't be easier. Green is mainstream now. And building green, once an idea on the margins of home building construction, is now not only accepted, but people seem to understand the logic behind it. People understand that saving resources and energy is smart, both for the planet our children will inherit, as well as for us today. It makes our homes more comfortable, livable, long-lasting, and cheaper to heat, cool, and maintain.

The more we learn about conserving energy and resources, the better prefab looks. All homes will one day be prefabricated. It simply makes more sense than approaching construction the way we currently do: dumping piles of lumber onto muddy lots and, one board at a time, nailing the parts together (all the while leaving materials open to the elements). Imagine building cars this way: A truck shows up with crates of parts and, a week later, a crew of mechanics arrive to slowly assemble the car in your driveway. There's a good reason cars are built on an assembly line.

And there's no denying the impact construction, has on our environment—depleting resources and filling landfills. We cut down far too many trees from far too many unmanaged forests, reducing the earth's ability to absorb carbon dioxide, which ultimately augments global warming. We've wasted energy, materials, and precious time using these methods.

Remember when the things we owned were meant to last? When jelly jars became drinking glasses? When we repaired broken toasters and televisions instead of trashing them? Somehow, it got too easy to discard the old and to buy a new one. However, recently, with growing awareness of global warming and the general state of the environment, people have been demanding that it be easier to conserve.

Grocery stores offer reusable bags. Car companies are improving energy-efficiency in cars and offering them at increasingly affordable prices every year. Lightbulbs give more light, last longer, and use less electricity. And investment in the technology and availability of sustainable, energy-efficient building materials is becoming more of an investment than a simple cost.

In this section you'll find all sorts of prefab houses, such as the 468 House and the Contemporary Farmhouse, which were built of prefab Structural Insulated Panels, or SIPs. These state-of-the-art building components go together tightly to insulate, stop air leaks, create indoor comfort, and dramatically reduce energy costs.

Modular houses, like the Tucker Bayou house, and panelized houses, such as the Tall + Narrow House, substantially reduce material waste and are built better and to tighter tolerances. The Artist Studio & Residence is a terrific example of how a commercial prefabricated product can be used to build a very efficient house.

Timber frames are composed of wood timbers crafted and fitted together in a factory. Because they are built indoors, these frames avoid exposure to weather. The Barn and A House of Straw demonstrate the beauty achievable using timber frame construction. These frames will hold up for generations, but even when their time eventually comes, the wood will be totally recyclable.

Workers used straw bales—which are generally considered waste—to form the comfortably thick walls of A House of Straw. As a result, the house consumes its energy by the teaspoon.

The steel frame used in the Eastbourne House not only contains a large percentage of recycled steel, but at the end of its life cycle, even that steel can, in turn, be recycled into something else.

Add to the advantages of prefabrication the following: modern home heating, cooling, moisture control, and insulation systems; ENERGY STAR appliances; a fuller understanding of building science; and a multitude of other home improvements both high-tech and low. You begin to realize that we've turned a corner, and what an improvement prefabrication is compared to the old and wasteful site-built, throw-away houses of the past.

Today the shades of green are unlimited. Houses can have a few basic green features or can be built nearly totally self-sustaining—even off the energy grid altogether.

Contemporary Farmhouse

Structural Insulated Panels (SIPs)

PHOTOGRAPHER:

Eric Roth Photography

(unless otherwise noted)

MANUFACTURER:

Winterpanel

ARCHITECT:

Christian Brown, Christian Brown Design

BUILDER:

Leach Construction of Vermont, LLC

LOCATION:

Jericho, Vermont

SIZE:

2,600 square feet

RATINGS:

ENERGY STAR—five star plus

GREEN ASPECTS:

Passive solar design

ICF (Insulating Concrete Form) foundation

Fiber cement siding

ENERGY STAR windows

ENERGY STAR appliances and lighting

High-efficiency heating system

Direct-vented gas fireplaces

Heat recovery ventilator

Standing-seam metal roof

Wheatboard cabinetry

Resin doors made from post-industrial reclaimed material

Bamboo flooring

Rubber flooring

Ecoresin panels for kitchen cabinets

Low-VOC (Volatile Organic Compound) paint finishes

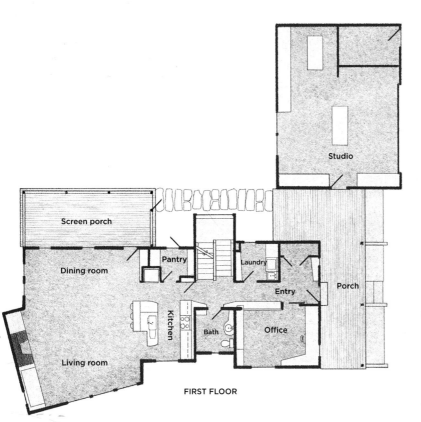

FIRST FLOOR

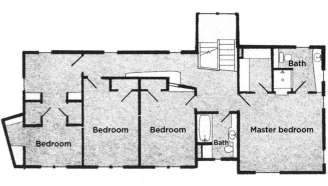

SECOND FLOOR

The house was oriented for maximum solar gain and to leave as many trees as possible undisturbed. Trees within the footprint of the house were dug up and and replanted. All plants are native and require minimal water.

When it came time to design a house for his own family, architect Christian Brown faced the hardest-to-please client of his career—himself. He wanted his own home to be beautiful, highly energy efficient, contemporary in design, but not so modern that it wouldn't fit in with the traditional regional style of rural Vermont. Thus he decided to build a contemporary farmhouse.

A Composition in Green

Christian was amazed by the variety of green building materials that were available, and realized that designing his own house would provide an excellent opportunity for experimentation. In his workshop, out back behind the house, he fabricated many of the interior elements for the house using these new materials.

With energy efficiency as his top priority, Christian knew that the choices of materials for the "shell," or the exterior envelope of the house, were critical. The foundation he chose was Insulated Concrete Form (ICF) (see Insulated Concrete Form Foundations sidebar, opposite), which created a heavily insulated, waterproof, and airtight basement, with a temperature variance of only a degree or two throughout the year.

Christian decided that the outer walls should be SIPS, because of their strength, excellent energy performance, and environmental friendliness. SIPS create little waste, provide a beefy R-38 insulating capacity (an excellent ability to resist the escape of heat) and are made from oriented strand board, which is manufactured using small-diameter, fast-growing trees, rather than mature trees.

Christian produced computer generated designs for the house and submitted them to his local SIPs manufacturer, Winterpanel. There, computer-controlled high-tech machines cut window and door openings in each finished panel. The SIPs were delivered to the site on a flatbed truck. Leach Construction put the panels together and topped the house off with a roof of 2 x 12 lumber insulated with R-50 closed-cell foam insulation.

Unlike an average house, a structure this tight doesn't leak air, and therefore needed mechanical ventilation to exhaust moisture and stale air and draw in fresh air. Fortunately, a heat recovery ventilator (see Heat and Energy Recovery Ventilation Systems sidebar, page 85) does all this, while also saving (recovering) the heat from the expelled air.

For roofing, Leach Construction installed a durable standing-seam metal roof. Red and brown fiber cement clapboards and panels (see Fiber Cement Siding sidebar, page 233) cover the exterior. This material is fire-, moisture-, and impact-resistant, in addition to being extremely durable.

Experimenting with New Materials

In the kitchen, Christian built concrete countertops (see Concrete Countertops sidebar, opposite) for the first time. It was a challenge building the forms because of all the curves in the design, but Christian appreciated the opportunity to

OPPOSITE ABOVE Forms fit together like Legos, assembled in rows with the windows and doors cut out to form the ICF foundation. (Photographs by homeowner)

OPPOSITE BELOW The house was oriented for maximum solar gain and to leave as many trees as possible undisturbed. Trees within the footprint of the house were dug up and replanted. All plants are native and require minimal water.

Insulated Concrete Form Foundations

ICFs are reinforced Styrofoam forms, or molds, into which concrete is poured. These are stacked, held together by plastic or metal connectors and, as in a traditional foundation, steel rebar is placed inside the forms before the concrete is poured. The Styrofoam is left in place and once the concrete cures, the outside is waterproofed and the interior is covered with drywall. The result is a strong, airtight, well-insulated, and waterproof foundation. The density of the concrete keeps basement temperatures stable. ICF concrete often contains a high content of recycled fly-ash, a residue produced during the combustion of coal at coal-fired electrical plants. The rebar is made from eighty percent recycled steel. ICFs are quickly assembled and allow for a high indoor air quality thanks to the watertight walls. To learn more, visit www.forms.org.

Rubber Flooring

The rubber flooring used in the master bathroom and main entryway contains recycled rubber made in a process that uses a minimal amount of water and little or no heat. The flooring is low in VOC emissions, extremely durable, nonflammable, available in lots of colors, and less expensive than many other flooring materials. Christian says it is not slippery when wet, and practically indestructible. To learn more, visit www.Ecosurfaces.com.

Concrete Countertops

Concrete is practical, versatile, and can be customized in an infinite number of ways with a combination of grinding, polishing, stamping, staining, and imbedding objects. The ancient material (the Romans built with it) is also less expensive than many other types of countertop materials and can adapt to any style of kitchen or bath. Plenty of instructions are available for do-it-yourselfers. Christian bought colors and mix for his concrete countertop from Cheng Design Products. He chose concrete because of its earthy appeal, reassuring density, and ease of customization. To learn more, visit www.chengdesign.com.

Christian fabricated the stairs from Laminated Strand Lumber (LSL), which he sanded thoroughly and finished with a urethane sealer. The engineered lumber is incredibly strong, saved him money, and has a unique look. The handrails are cherry wood with stainless steel cables.

BELOW Except for the upholstered pieces, Christian built all the living room furniture. The fixed, or inoperable, windows were designed to open the house to the beautiful views while not impeding them. The awning windows below, open for ventilation. Here the flooring is bamboo, a highly renewable material.

customize their color, shape, and design. He had aluminum scraps that were found at a scrapyard embedded into the concrete countertops for visual interest.

Christian chose wheatboard, a product made from recycled wheat straw, to handcraft the kitchen cabinets and built-ins throughout the house. Panels made with strands of wild grasses pressed between sheets of a translucent resin were inset into the kitchen cabinet doors and the divider that separates the living room from his home office. Christian selected an engineered material—laminated strand lumber—for the stairs. People generally use this material for heavy framing, and rarely as an exposed surface, but Christian was not deterred. He sanded it thoroughly and finished it with a water-based urethane. The results speak for themselves: The treads and stringers (the sides of stairs) cost far less than if they'd been built with finish lumber, and the stairs are incredibly strong and have a terrific look that is both rustic and contemporary. To highlight the stairway, Christian decided on cherry wood handrails and stainless steel cable rails.

In the entrance and master bathroom, floors are a colorful rubber, which Christian sought out because it is immensely eco-friendly (see Rubber Flooring sidebar, page 25). Even with three small children in the house, these floors have proven to be virtually indestructible. What is more, they are comfortable to the foot and do not get slippery when wet.

Comfort and Light

Christian oriented the house in such a way that would best capture sunlight and aligned it with a long stretch of tall pines on the property, which make a beautiful backdrop. Large roof overhangs block the high summer sun but let the lower winter sun shine inside. The overhangs also allow the family to leave windows open even when it rains.

Thanks to its solar orientation and narrow footprint, the family rarely has to turn the lights on during the day. Christian was careful to plan the lighting scheme with many task lights, situating light just where needed (which saves electricity), instead of installing larger fixtures as general lighting. Because the house is built so tight and energy efficient, the family's electric bill is very low compared to similar size houses in the area.

Jutting out at the rear of the house is the stair tower, which includes highly efficient, top-to-bottom Kalwall panels. These panels are thick sandwiches of reinforced, translucent fiberglass with insulating material in between, which let in lots of light without sacrificing energy efficiency. Christian likes the panels because they form what looks like a huge shoji screen.

The stairs have no risers, so the abundant light streaming through the Kalwal panels is able to pass into the house. The family leaves two hopper windows at the top of the tower open from April through October, as they are protected from the elements by the deep overhang. The stair tower acts as a chimney, letting hot air rise up and out, providing the house with a natural cooling source.

To heat the first two floors, Christian had hydronic radiant floor heating (see Hydronic vs. Electric Radiant Heating sidebar, page 125) installed. To save money, radiators heat the top floor. The water for both hydronic systems is warmed by a small, on-demand boiler, which satisfies all the hot water needs of the family, though it's only the size of a small suitcase. A super insulated holding tank can prioritize water distribution for showering, rather than for other uses. A direct-vented gas fireplace in the living room provides extra heat on the coldest Vermont winter days.

OPPOSITE ABOVE LEFT Chris incorporated junkyard aluminum scraps into the kitchen countertop. He said the biggest challenge he faced in creating the countertop was making curves in the forms.

OPPOSITE ABOVE RIGHT The countertops are made of concrete. The flooring is an eco-friendly rubber, which Christian says is nonslip and indestructible.

OPPOSITE BELOW The kitchen cabinets are made of wheatboard, a plywood-type material made out of ground wheat stalks bound together with a formaldehyde-free resin. Strands of grass are inset within the layers for an earthy, natural look. Christian also made the concrete countertops and added stainless-steel tiles as a backdrop.

OVERLEAF LEFT ABOVE Workers lift a SIP wall into place with the help of aluminum wall jack, an apparatus that allows builders to lift much larger sections of wall than they could by hand. (Photograph by homeowner)

OVERLEAF LEFT BELOW Christian designed these rusted planters, and his neighbor constructed them. These plants, as well as those in the rest of the landscape, are native to the area.

OVERLEAF RIGHT Connected to the house by an open walkway is the workshop/garage. The stair tower jutting out on the rear includes an insulated translucent panel that lets in light without sacrificing energy.

A Work in Progress

It was a dream come true for Christian to design and build a house for his own family. The end result of his self-described "relentless curiosity" is a house that is a compelling and attractive mix. Its SIPs walls, textures, colors, and creative design come together to form a home that is, inside and out, an extremely energy-efficient and sustainable home structure.

Tucker Bayou

Modular

PHOTOGRAPHER:

Jack Gardner (unless otherwise noted)

ARCHITECT:

Chris Haley, Project Architect,

Looney Ricks Kiss Architects, Inc.

MANUFACTURER:

Haven Custom Homes

BUILDER:

The St. Joe Company

LOCATION:

WaterSound, Florida

SIZE:

3,000 square feet

GREEN ASPECTS:

Fiber cement siding

High-efficiency windows

ENERGY STAR appliances

On-demand water heater

Low-VOC (Volatile Organic Compound) paint

Large overhangs

Screened porches

High-efficiency HVAC (heating, ventilating, and air conditioning)

Native plants

Moisture-resistant cement board in bathrooms

Detached garage

Bathroom exhaust fans and clothes dryers ducted to outside

ENERGY STAR ceiling fans

Engineered reclaimed flooring

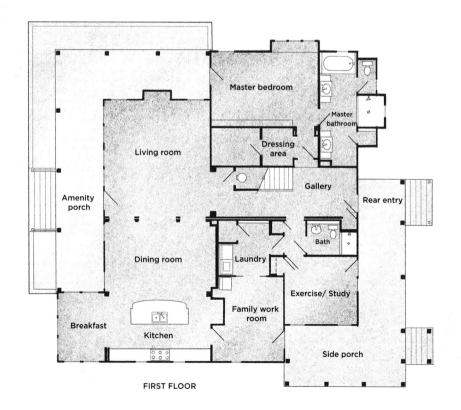

FIRST FLOOR

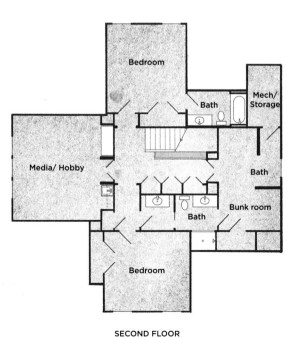

SECOND FLOOR

If you think a modular house is another name for a mobile home, meet the Tucker Bayou house. Mobile homes are boring boxes and this house is anything but. Wrapped inside a traditional Southern façade is a structure that exemplifies contemporary luxury, energy efficiency, and down-home, comfortable, country design.

Southern Living magazine approached the St. Joe Company, a Florida developer, to build an "Idea House" in WaterSound, a coastal development. And thus, plans began for what would eventually become the Tucker Bayou house. St. Joe was commissioned to build the house using standard on-site construction. But time was short, so St. Joe hired Haven Custom Homes to manufacture the house as a modular. Haven has a reputation for speed and efficiency, even when it comes to custom-made houses. And at Water-Sound the house had to go up fast while also meeting the strict design guidelines of the chic development.

The Design Challenge

Any house that is going to be built in WaterSound must be approved by a design review board that ensures that homes meet stringent design standards. These guidelines cover everything from roof slope to window style to interior finishes. Because the Tucker Bayou house was intended to be a show home for a style-setting national magazine and one of the first houses built in WaterSound, it had to meet and set particularly high standards.

Haven's Steve Bassett recalled that "the house was 'modularized' in a conference room" in about two hours. "The modular version was 42 square feet larger than the original plan with none of the original design features sacrificed." The only difference would be that in the places where the modules come together, the walls would be wider. They call these "marriage walls."

Yet because of design complexities and community guidelines, challenges arose, especially in the complex roof design. Ultimately, eight modules of varying width had to marry up at different roof angles. Inside the house, the finish materials and architectural millwork required by the design guidelines "pushed our craftsmen to the limit," Bassett said.

Project Architect Chris Haley, of Looney Ricks Kiss Architects, enjoyed the challenge, and looked forward to overturning the common misconception of a modular house as being relatively equivalent to a mobile home. When the house was complete, Chris challenged guests to find the seams where the modules had been married; nobody did. Not only was there no sacrifice of design or quality, but the house went up on schedule with a minimum of waste.

Since Tucker Bayou is designed to be either a permanent or second home for active retired adults, the master bedroom is on the first floor. An upstairs bunkroom with multiple beds accommodates visiting children or grandchildren. A second bedroom suite upstairs does nicely for a visiting adult couple.

OPPOSITE ABOVE The eight modules of the house were carefully lifted into place and bolted together without disturbing the property's many trees. (Photo by Steve Bassett)

OPPOSITE BELOW The rear of the house faces the street, where people who are driving there might enter. The front of the house is on the golf course and the entrance, traditionally used by people in the community.

A Resurgence of Ceiling Fans

Ceiling fans create wind that, in turn, carries heat away from the body, driving down the body temperature. Conversely, if nobody's in the room, nobody's being cooled off, so fans churning in an empty room just waste electricity. Fans run counterclockwise in the warm summer. Most fans can run in reverse in the winter, producing an updraft, forcing warm air near the ceiling down below where the people are. If used correctly, ceiling fans lower air conditioning and heating costs. They now come in as many styles as any other fixture in the house. Ceiling fans also have a variety of speeds, blade pitch, and controls, and some come with remote controls. Ceiling fans with light kits that are ENERGY STAR–rated are about 50 percent more efficient than conventional fan/light units and save more than 15 dollars per year on energy costs. Units with only a fan will save 10 dollars per year.

Why Modular

Built indoors under strict supervision and quality control, modular homes decidedly speed up the on-site construction process, eliminating about two-thirds of the time it takes to build a conventional home. Once on site, workers assemble the modules quickly so as to protect the interior of the house from damaging weather conditions. Environmentally speaking, modular construction generates about half the waste of on-site construction. As an added bonus, many of the materials used in a modular factory are recycled in the factory. Workers often live close to a modular plant, which cuts down on commuting fuel use. Futhermore, they can work on multiple houses each day without traveling from site to site. Because materials are kept indoors, they don't get wet or mildew. Most exciting is that with modular construction, you can build a beautiful, custom home, much like the Tucker Bayou house—a far cry from the tacky boxes of just a decade or so ago.

In the kitchen, the appliances are all ENERGY STAR–rated. The windows are not only energy efficient, but provide magnificent views of the local habitat.

BELOW Amazing built-in bunk beds save space and make sleeping over an adventure for kids or grownups. Those who decide to sleep in the lower bunks also get individual flat-screen televisions.

BOTTOM French doors lead from the master bedroom to a small private patio, where one can enjoy a morning cup of coffee.

From concept to move-in-ready, the house took twenty-three weeks to complete. Six of those weeks were devoted to coordinating the players involved with the show house and to producing final, working drawings. Haven Custom Homes built the house in its factory in just eight weeks. It took one week to deliver the house, set it, and make it watertight (the house was roughly 70 percent complete on delivery). Site work, and indoor/outdoor trim and finish work took two months.

The Environmental Challenge

WaterSound is an environmentally conscious community with stringent habitat and tree-preservation standards. Therefore, Haven Custom Homes had to exercise particular care with its crane, both to prevent erosion and minimize disturbance of the many mature trees on the property. When they completed construction, the only trees Haven had removed were those within the footprint of the house. The modules were "dropped" into place with minimal disruption. Remarkably, the construction process yielded less than one dumpster of job-site waste (a typical dumpster holds 20 cubic yards; the typical amount of waste from building a house this size would be 75 cubic yards).

Drought can be a problem in the Water-Sound area, so the development requires most plants around new houses to be native to the area. Local plants have evolved to deal with drought and to resist pests, reducing the need for watering and pest-killing chemicals.

Even more subtle efforts were made to ease Tucker Bayou's carbon footprint. The windows had to provide views, blanket the house in balanced natural light, and avoid solar gain (which would have increased cooling costs in the summer). The designers accomplished all objectives:

The Beauty of a Screened Porch

Screened porches have been popular for about a century. But widespread use of air conditioning has, over the years, diminished the number of new homes built with porches. Thankfully, they are making a big comeback. A porch is a great place to cool off on a hot day or to relax under a soft breeze. But they also save electricity in another way. A porch that is on the south, east, or west side of the house shades those windows and exterior walls, keeping them cool and protecting the material from the elements.

Detach the Garage

Cars give off carbon monoxide, and common garage items like paint, paint thinner, and paint remover evaporate. These fumes have to go somewhere, and it had better not be into the house. Detaching the garage from the living space keeps air free of harmful pollutants. Several green certification programs, such as LEED-H, give multiple points to homes with detached garages or no garage at all, because of the health benefits.

BELOW A screened porch extends living space and creates a comfortable and energy-free place to enjoy nature or neighbors.

BOTTOM Separating the garage from the house prevents the permeation of dangerous fumes into living spaces.

The front porch is a great place to relax and unwind and offers an outdoor space lit by the sun and cooled by the breeze.

OPPOSITE LEFT The blackboard/cork-board panel in the multipurpose room keeps things organized while hiding the electrical panel.

OPPOSITE RIGHT The multipurpose room, located between the kitchen and the laundry room, cuts down on clutter that would otherwise pile up. The metal table is a great place to cut flowers and set down groceries.

RIGHT An open floor plan, perfect for casual entertaining, also allows air to flow throughout the house. The ceiling fan in the living room does its part by gently stirring the air and helping cool the occupants during the warm months.

The house has views of the beautiful golf course, large overhangs that protect the interior from solar gain, and energy efficient windows (filled with low-E, argon gas) that keep the interior cool in the summer and warm in winter. Ceiling fans throughout the house cut down on air conditioning. A screened porch offers outdoor relaxation cooled by the breeze.

Air quality was also important. The paints, adhesives, and other finishes were low-VOC (Volatile Organic Compounds) (Reducing VOCs sidebar, page 177) to keep the air clean. A detached garage ensures that auto carbon monoxide stays out of the house. The stove range hood, bathroom fans, and clothes dryer all vent directly outside, reducing mold and mildew.

Lowering Maintenance

Reducing the need for repainting, refinishing, replanting, or replacing are key objectives of environmental design. At Tucker Bayou, all involved parties made an effort to reduce the carbon footprint of the house and to keep future maintenance low.

Native plants (see Native Landscaping sidebar, page 63) reduce irrigation requirements. Fiber cement siding resists rot, fungus, termites, fire, and that other dependable Florida menace: hurricanes and their high wind. The downstairs flooring is made of a layer of reclaimed heart pine (a beautiful and durable material prized for centuries) bonded to a layer of FSC (Forest Stewardship Council)–certified (see What FSC Is All About sidebar, page 102) spruce, pine, and fir. The finish is a penetrating oil made from cold-pressed vegetable oils and aromatic hardening oils, which exceed the most stringent standards for VOCs.

High-efficiency windows and heating and cooling systems, ENERGY STAR appliances, and fans lower energy use. The on-demand water heater wastes less energy when not in use than ordinary water heaters.

Artist Studio + Residence

Steel insulated panels and steel frame

ARCHITECT:

Olle Lundberg, Lundberg Design

CONTRACTOR:

Malpas and Birmingham Inc.

LANDSCAPE ARCHITECT:

Kikuchi and Associates

LOCATION:

San Francisco, California

SIZE:

4,655 square feet

GREEN ASPECTS:

Steel framing

Prefinished and prefabricated panel system

Concrete slab floors

Hydronic radiant heating

FSC-certified woods

Dual-flush toilets

Solar panel wiring

Passive solar

Low-E (Low-Emissivity) glass

Natural ventilation

No HVAC

Drought-tolerant planting

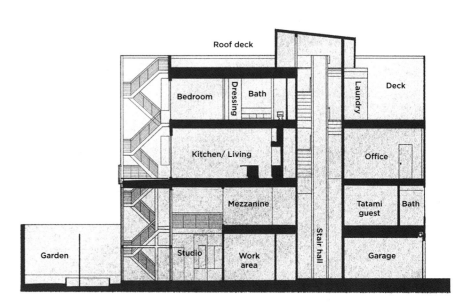

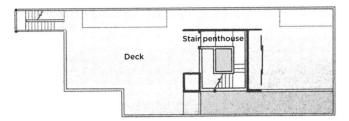

ROOF

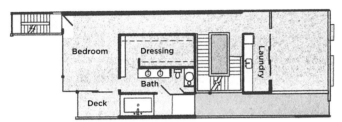

FOURTH FLOOR

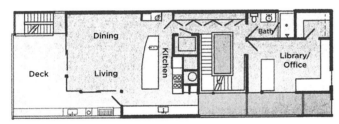

THIRD FLOOR

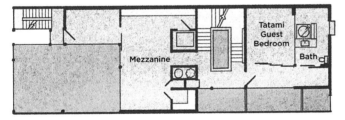

SECOND FLOOR

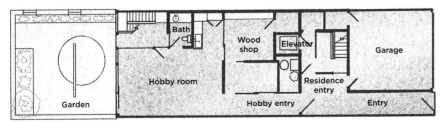

FIRST FLOOR

OPPOSITE This is what the property looked like before John and Dana bought it. While the space wasn't livable, the house at 55 Sheridan Street served as a studio for artists Jonah Roll and Brian Groggin in which they created *Desire for the Other*, a large-scale sculpture commissioned by the San Jose Museum of Art in California. Unfortunately, this 1916 warehouse had to be demolished because it was found to be structurally unsound on the shaky San Andreas soil. (Photo by anonymous.)

BELOW Three sides of the house are constructed with insulated steel sandwich panels; the southern exposure is mostly glass. To accommodate the artist in residence, Olle Lundberg designed and fabricated 10 foot front and rear doors, which John Dunham describes as something out of the *Wizard of Oz*. (Photo by Michelle Kriebel)

John Dunham and his wife, artist Dana Kawano, considered themselves lucky to find the old, rundown, and abused brick and stucco building. From the first look, they could see right through the building's cracks, graffiti, and peeling paint to what it *could* become. Not so much of a mental leap given that the old paint warehouse was situated in the artsy, industrial SoMa (South of Market Street) district, on a street lined with some residential lofts (and a local coffee roastery, auto mechanics, and a car wash). The couple had always wanted to live in the heart of San Francisco. A modern newly constructed, contemporary home replacing the dilapidated old building would give them just that—along with a workshop for John and studio space large enough for Dana's art, which ranges from paintings and pastels to large stone sculptures.

The house would blend the industrial grit of their new neighborhood with an attitude of ecological friendliness and energy efficiency, especially relevant in San Francisco, the first city in the country to ban plastic grocery bags.

Four-Story Glory

John and Dana searched for an architect with experience building in San Francisco, someone who could navigate the stringent permit process as well as understand their vision. They also wanted to build four floors up to take advantage of views, light, and the open air that the height would afford them.

Olle Lundberg of Lundberg Design fit the bill. He designed the couple a four-story, 50 foot-tall house made of prefabricated steel panels that would adhere to the minimal, "yet modern Asian" aesthetic John and Dana were after. Olle fabricated a few elements—such as oversized entrance doors to accommodate Dana's artwork—in his nearby studio.

In addition to steel, concrete was another major building material Olle used. The floors throughout the house, the garden pond, and the walls are concrete. Concrete is inexpensive, versatile, and useful in regulating indoor temperature. In addition, with concrete floors, they could install radiant floor heating, a source of natural, energy-efficient heat. When it's chilly, the dense concrete floor absorbs the sun's heat and slowly and comfortably radiates that free energy back into the house after dark (see Concrete Floors: The Hot and Cold of Them sidebar, opposite).

Not Your Typical Panels

John and Dana's first vision for the house was a sleek, modern design, composed of steel, concrete, and glass. Though from the get-go they fully expected that these materials would be too expensive, and they would ultimately have to go with a less expensive design using steel and wood. So it was an especially good day for them when, during the design process, Olle concluded that steel, concrete, and glass would work at little extra cost. The house would be clean and durable, and reflect the minimal, modern look they wanted. Added benefits of steel and concrete would include security against the inevitable next earthquake, straighter walls, and a unified look

The garden, designed by Kikuchi and Associates, has a tranquil, Asian influence. They designed it to look interesting not only from the ground level, but also from the floors above. (Photo by Ryan Hughes)

Concrete Floors: The Hot and Cold of Them

Sunshine and concrete floors make a lovely couple, especially when it comes to inexpensively regulating the temperature inside a house. If insulated from the ground and significantly exposed to direct winter sunlight, a concrete floor will soak up heat during the day and release it at night (called "solar gain"). In this house, Olle designed and positioned the windows to allow as much of the sun's heat as possible to be absorbed by the floors. In summer, when the sun is higher in the sky, the floors are mostly shielded, so the house stays cool. The radiant floor heating system does double-duty in the summer when its piping is filled with chilled water. Heating and cooling a house this way also improves air quality, because unlike a forced air system, there's nothing blowing dust and pollutants through the air. Radiant heating systems also make zoning simpler because each room can be controlled individually.

A Breath of Fresh Air

Ventilation is crucial to a healthy home environment, particularly when the house is as airtight as John and Dana's. Fans, air purifiers, and air exchangers are the typical mechanical ventilation methods, but natural ventilation is best. Natural ventilation uses less energy and doesn't require much beyond good planning. John and Dana's home has several methods of natural ventilation. The house is oriented with solar gain and air circulation in mind. Almost the entire east side of the house is glass with operable windows to take advantage of breezes and sunlight. At the top of the four-story staircase is an operable exterior door, which acts as an exhaust chimney, sucking hot air up and out. The plan works: Their first summer was one of the hottest on record, but the couple stayed comfortable without air conditioning.

Dana Kawano designed the interior. Rooms on the southern, rear side of the house require minimal lighting during the day because of the floor-to-ceiling windows. (Photo by Ryan Hughes)

BELOW With a generally neutral palette, there are surprise colors such as red on the kitchen stools and the red walls in the living rooms. (Photo by Ryan Hughes)

BOTTOM The Tatami room serves as a guest room for lucky visitors to this beautiful stunning city home. The floor is covered with tatami mats, while shoji screens close off the room. There are no visible beds in the room, but John and Dana store a futon in an oversized closet outside the room. (Photo by Ryan Hughes)

undiluted by the use of too many materials. In a city with a history of earthquakes and fires, John says that his concrete and steel house feels reassuringly substantial.

The prefabricated steel panels that Olle selected for the house façade are an unusual choice for a residence. These panels are often used on commercial buildings, which tend to be supported by a steel frame, a rare skeleton for a house. The advantages of panels for this project are their industrial appearance, energy efficiency, and quick and simple installation.

The panels are made of galvanized steel (steel coated with a thin layer of zinc to resist corrosion), each with a thick, insulating, rockwool core made from "slag" waste (waste from the iron-smelting process). The recycled slag is spun into five-inch-thick, fire-resistant fibers, which are three times more energy efficient than typical fiberglass. They have a high R-value—the standard measurement of insulation, or resistance to the transfer of heat—of 41. Also beneficial is that workers can install the panels in hours with a forklift.

The panels have a "one-hour fire-rating," meaning they offer more than one hour's worth of protection. The core materials are non-toxic and recyclable. Because the house is tightly flanked on both sides by other buildings, fire-rated panels were a requirement. (The panels on the front of the house are similar to the fire-rated panels, but have an insulating, urethane core.)

Using prefabricated panels greatly reduced the on-site waste that typically builds up during construction. Having these panels also decreased the need for drywall in the studio, where silky steel gives the desired industrial look. John and Dana like the raw appearance of the panels, and so the couple decided to leave them exposed in the ground-floor studio and on the mezzanine level. But they added drywall on the upper levels to provide for wall treatments and color.

Natural Ventilation

San Francisco weather tends to be chilly, with brief, occasional periods of brutal heat. Yet from the start, Dana and John wanted nothing to do with the whirring and clicking of a forced-air, central air conditioning, or heating system. Accordingly, the house is the quiet and calming oasis they sought out.

The inspired and informed design of the house made doing without an HVAC system practically effortless (see A Breath of Fresh Air sidebar, page 45). The southern face is almost entirely glass, filling the house with light and air. As the air warms inside the house, it rises and exits through a door at the top of the stairs, drawing in cooler air through the many operable windows and creating a constant, fresh, cooling effect. Their first summer in the house was one of the hottest on record, but John and Dana stayed perfectly comfortable without noisy and expensive air conditioning.

In winter, radiant heat rises from the hot-water-fed, or "hydronic," tubes, buried in the concrete floors, to comfortably warm the house. Forced air, on the other hand, tends to leave some areas overheated and others too cool, while radiant heat rising up from the floor evenly distributes warmth. The energy-efficient gas boiler sends hot water through the floor and provides household hot water.

A Private Retreat

In many places, the architectural design of John and Dana's blends indoors with the outdoors. In order to best take advantage of this, they called on Kikuchi and Associates to create a landscape design that would soften and counter the strict angularity of the house, while contributing to the existing Eastern Asian aesthetic. The resulting garden is itself a form of sculpture that looks as lovely from the ground as it does from the upper floors. Large, sleek expanses of raw concrete, formed into curves and angles, are nicely balanced out by delicate greenery and the softening effect of a small pond and waterfall that Kikuchi and Associates designed. The plants are native and drought-tolerant, and add color and life to the serene retreat. An outdoor kitchen lets Dana and John fully use the space.

BELOW The large windows in the studio flood the space with light, while visually connecting the room to the beautiful gardens just beyond. (Photo by John Dunham)

OPPOSITE The master bedroom, like many of the spaces in the house, has a small deck for extending the interior space to the outside. (Photo by Dana Kawano)

The Barn

Panelized and timber frame

PHOTOGRAPHER:

Roger Wade Studio;
construction photos by Rose and
Bear Home Builders

MANUFACTURER:

Bear Creek Timberwrights

DESIGNER:

Robert Berlin

BUILDER:

Rose and Bear Home Builders

LANDSCAPING:

Bear Paw Landscaping

LOCATION:

Gallatin Gateway, Montana

SQUARE FOOTAGE:

1,440 square feet

GREEN ASPECTS:

Passive solar

Living roof

Steel roof

Hydronic radiant heating

Cement floors

Reclaimed granite and timber

Bamboo floors

Energy-efficient windows

Compact-fluorescent (CFL) lighting

Smart Home System

Vintage furniture

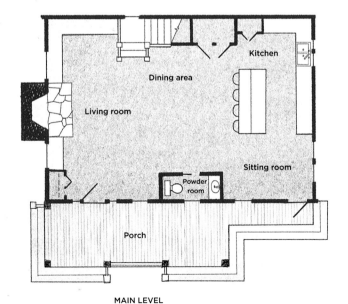

MAIN LEVEL

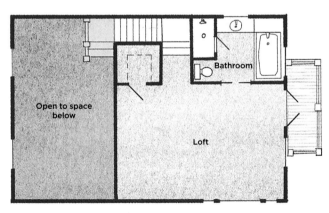

LOFT

The living roof is set in an 8-inch box with 6 inches of soil. Drains at the front of the box allow the release of excess water during intense periods of thaw or heavy rainfall. The native Montana wild grasses and wildflowers were originally planted off-site, and then later transferred to the roof for planting.

Montana couple Heather and Robert Berlin couldn't be more "big city." She's from Boston; he's from New York. But early in their relationship, something inside drew them West and deep into Big Sky country. They saw themselves as a couple of urban cowboys traveling to cowboy country, yet holding onto their big city sensibilities. They ended up near Yellowstone, where they started their own construction company, Rose and Bear Home Builders. At first they built homes for other people. But it wasn't long before Robert was ready to build a house for themselves.

The plan was to build a modest, green house in the Montana hills that reflected their East Coast, urban upbringing. In October 2004, they bought property. Four months later, it looked like a house. As a designer, Robert had a fairly tight design sketched before they even owned the property. It was a house, he said, of "clean lines and an integrity of material, with prebuilt items used to detail the space in a high-style fashion." They wanted it to look very Montana on the outside, but East-Coast on the inside.

His company prefabricated panels that fit to form the precision parts of his first-floor plan. For the second floor, Bear Creek Timberwrights crafted a loft and roof system using timber framing. Four months later, Heather and Robert moved in.

They wanted the exterior to look natural between the rugged Montana hills and the wild Gallatin River. The interior would reflect their lives back East: clean, urban, and loft-like. The tradi-tional barn style would blend in with the surroundings, particularly with that of the family living to the north who breed Belgian draft horses. Once the house was built, the Berlins felt content inside their house and out.

Mixing Prefab with Energy Efficiency

It snowed when Heather and Robert closed on the land that October. And it continued snowing through their April move-in. But thanks to panelized construction, Robert quickly built the first floor, even through the snowy days. Panels made the work go quickly, and kept costs down. On a construction site, time really is money. The second floor timber frame was built in nearby Victor, and three months after he ordered it, Robert's crew raised the frame right up to the big sky.

Robert had always been concerned with energy efficiency and responsible use of resources. It was an attitude he followed up with action, an attitude that was just beginning to be known as "green building." Though no green rating systems existed at the time, Robert intuitively chose reclaimed and recycled materials when possible, made sure the houses he designed were tight and energy efficient, and always took steps to minimize the impact his houses made on the environment. When it came time to build their house, Robert poured on the green.

Using passive heating and cooling, heavy insulation, a tightly sealed "building envelope" (the exterior shell of the house), and high-efficiency windows well-placed to take advantage

LEFT The finishings are more "big-city," while the exterior is more country.

BELOW After the panelized system was complete, the second-floor walls and roof timber frame were set. (Photograph by Rose and Bear Home-Builders)

BOTTOM First-floor panels had been set, and the timber frame erected to form the second floor. (Photograph by Rose and Bear Home-Builders)

Robert Berlin always had an affinity for barn doors, so he incorporated them into the entrances of the sitting room and garage.

BELOW The split door in the kitchen allows natural breezes to circulate throughout the house without letting the dogs loose.

BOTTOM Covered by a living roof, the porch is a very comfortable place to sit and enjoy Montana. In the winter, when the sun is low, the light ducks below the porch overhang and peers into the windows to add passive solar energy to the house. In summertime the porch keeps out the sun.

A Living Roof

Ordinarily, something growing on the roof is cause for concern. On the south-facing porch of Robert and Heather's house, a living roof was the goal. While we tend to think of most things that are "green" as being cutting-edge, green roofs have been around for centuries. Inhabitants of the Great Plains called them sod roofs. Well before that, Scandinavians used living roofs to protect their timber homes. Today they're called green roofs or "eco-roofs," and they provide a layer of vegetation, in soil, over a waterproof membrane supported by wood framing.

Eco-roofs are aesthetically pleasing, add insulation, reduce outside noise, protect the roof from destructive ultraviolet radiation, filter pollution from rainwater, and absorb much of the water that could otherwise create runoff problems. In other words, they are remarkable. Green roofs can be very heavy, which means you have to have an extremely strong roof. However, cost savings come from the roof's insulating ability and from its extended life.

Several cities issue grants and tax incentives for the construction of green roofs. Annapolis, Maryland, offers tax credits; Chicago gives grants. You should check with local building officials regarding incentives and zoning restrictions for living roofs. (An excellent Web site for further information is www.greenroofs.com.)

A Mind of Its Own

Smart Home Systems can combine functions such as security, entertainment, lighting, and climate control into one little box, saving energy and sanity (for controls, one is better than many). A variety of sensors monitor temperature inside and outside to adjust heating/cooling, lower shades against solar gain, and dim lights when the sun brightens a room. Moisture sensors start fans or sump pumps. Occupancy sensors detect lack of activity and turn off lights.

These systems are also capable of more subtle functions. For instance, the Barn's hydronic system "knows" approximately how long it takes to heat the floor and calculates the perfect time to start the system based on feedback from sensors. The astronomical clock within the system calculates solar position, and sunrise and sunset at the house's latitude and longitude on any given day, which enables it to adjust and conserve heating. The system can operate outdoor sprinklers, and vary the length and frequency of watering by sensing humidity and rainfall conditions. But perhaps one of its most valuable functions is a panel that shows levels of carbon output, energy use, and cost. It turns out that when homeowners see their energy use, they tend to use less.

About Home Fire Sprinkler Systems

Living in a remote wilderness is paradise for some. But if your house catches on fire, it could be totally devastated by the time a fire truck arrives. If your home is far from a fire department, a heat-activated overhead sprinkler system may be your best bet. In modern systems, only sprinkler heads closest to the fire activate, releasing 15 to 20 gallons of water per minute (gpm), in contrast to the 250 gpm from a fire hose. So the fire can be doused at the outset without too much water damage. Although costs can be high—about 1 percent of the home's cost—some insurers offer discounts. To learn more, go to www.homefiresprinkler.org.

BELOW The warmth, beauty, craft, and strength of the timber frame are obvious in the master bedroom ceiling trusses.

BOTTOM Lovely bamboo flooring conceals the radiant heat beneath.

of the sun, Robert sought out ways to reduce his energy use. He recently became a LEED Accredited Professional and wants to pursue NAHB (National Association of Home Builders) accreditation as well. He'll continue to build green houses, but with a little more guidance than before.

The Barn is on an east-west axis in order to grab the maximum passive solar energy and the best views of the mountains and the river. Robert had expanding foam blown into the walls to insulate and seal off air, as air leaks are a huge source of energy loss. The tighter and more insulated the building envelope, the less he would need to spend on fuel. Concrete floors, tinted with several colors to create an interesting effect, absorb the sun's heat and help heat the house.

The windows in the Barn are high-tech; They are low-E coated, argon filled, double-paned, vacuum sealed, and coated with an interior film for phenomenal energy efficiency. The couple mixed it up with a variety of windows—awning, casements, fixed, and transom—each arranged just so, to take best advantage of sunlight and cool breezes. A slew of windows on the south side let sunshine pour in, keeping the house warm in winter. Come summer, the large, green, overhanging roof shades south-facing windows from excess solar gain. There is only one window on the north side of the house because that side gets far less sun. The roof over the porch is alive—a so-called living or "eco-roof" (see A Living Roof sidebar, page 55), which absorbs heat and turns it into something green, in this case actual vegetation.

The shape and design of the house encourages air circulation. Part of the lower level has a thirty-foot ceiling. In the colder months, warm air rises to the top and creates a warming convection. In the summertime, French doors in the loft open onto a deck, drawing air through the house and up and out, causing a cooling flow, like nature's air conditioning. Needless to say, minimal additional heating or cooling is needed.

However, this is Montana, where temperatures have been know to drop down to 30 degrees below zero in the dead of winter. So the Berlins installed a hydronic radiant heating system that's zoned to provide heat where it's needed, when it's needed. On a normal winter day, without the radiant heat, it can get so warm in the house that Robert says he occasionally has to open a few windows to cool down. On a typically colder day, though, the Smart Home System balances and blends interior temperatures through sensors installed around the house (See A Mind of Its Own sidebar, opposite).

Reduce, Reuse, Recycle

The Berlins were able to add a bit of history to their new barn. As it happened, a crumbling barn on an 1869 homestead in nearby Silver Star, was slated for demolition. When Robert found out, he had it dismantled and stored, and ended up incorporating many of its parts into his home and into other houses he built. The barn door on the first floor was crafted from lovely old wood salvaged from the structure. The hearth is built with granite from the barn's foundation. The mantle was shaped from a knee brace in the old barn frame. These old pieces tie the Berlins' new home to the land and its heritage.

"Returning home in the evening as the sun sets behind the Gallatin Mountains—and just a little bit of light remains as the night falls on Big Sky—I get to see the home that Heather and I built for ourselves. That coupled with the knowledge that the home is a reflection of our lives out West together, the lives we had before we met, and the future we make together, all of these elements are present as I turn the corner and head for home."

468 House

Structural Insulated Panels (SIPs)

ARCHITECT/PHOTOGRAPHER:

Jonathan Delcambre

MANUFACTURER:

FischerSIPs

BUILDER:

Ferrier Custom Homes

LOCATION:

Dallas, Texas

SIZE:

2,400 square feet

RATINGS:

ENERGY STAR

GREEN ASPECTS:

Infill lot

Passive solar design

ENERGY STAR windows and doors

ENERGY STAR appliances

Daylighting

Low VOC paints and stains

Tankless water heater

High-efficiency AC

High-efficiency heat pump

Direct-vent gas fireplace

Energy recovery ventilator (ERV)

Low-flow toilets

CFL lighting

Spray foam insulation

Recycled scrap lumber used as mulch

Pervious driveway material

Cabinetry from regionally harvested wood

TPO (Thermoplastic polyolefin membrane) roofing

Carpet pads and carpeting made from recycled fibers

Native landscaping

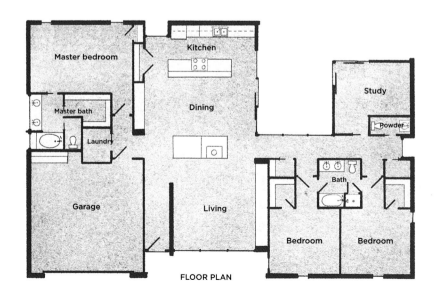

FLOOR PLAN

ABOVE Jon chose 16" emperor brick mixed with cedar siding for the facade of the house. The vinyl-clad windows are affordable, efficient, and well insulated against the noise of the middle school across the street. For the driveway and courtyards, Jon chose crushed granite, which allows rainwater to seep into the ground, eliminating storm water runoff.

LEFT The SIPs panels were quickly erected on the prepared foundation.

After working as a commercial architect in London and New York, Jonathan Delcambre settled in Dallas. Not to work on office buildings or museums, but to design houses. And not just any houses: modestly sized green houses in the style known as mid-century modern. All in Dallas, Texas, a major epicenter of McMansions.

The first house Jon designed was for his family, which includes his wife D'Lee and their two young daughters. He set out to build his version of a 1950s ranch house, streamlined and uncluttered, but with the latest technology to make it energy efficient and healthy for living. He also intended to show that a nice modern green home could also be relatively affordable too.

In a Good Place

As it happened, the couple inherited three small lots from D'Lee's grandfather—a Dallas builder in the 1960s and 1970s—in the Old Lake Highlands neighborhood. The lots were close to D'Lee's family, but Jon needed city permission to combine the three into a single building lot. In this desirable, old neighborhood, their options were limited: either build on the combined lots, or buy an existing house and do a teardown, which is a decidedly non-green way to go.

The neighborhood had even more attraction because of its close proximity to downtown Dallas, where Jon works, so his shorter commute would mean less time going somewhere and more time being somewhere. It would also cut down on driving costs.

It's also a great area for staying put. Nearby is White Rock Lake, twelve hundred acres of recreational opportunity, including sailing and bike trails.

Reducing Future Costs

Jon's number one goal was to prove that he could build an energy-efficient house spending more or less the same amount you would to build a conventional, non-energy-efficient house in the area. His final price came in at about $125 per square foot, which is less than half of what many non-green and non-energy-efficient houses in Dallas cost. And that figure doesn't factor in the long-term energy savings.

For the house's infrastructure—the bones of the house—Jon chose SIPs because they are precisely prefabricated to fit together tightly and in very little time on-site. As Jon explained, "the large panels allow for greater roof spans and open floor plans . . . reducing construction time, reducing material waste, and creating a tighter building envelope." Ferrier Custom Homes, a contractor with green and energy-efficient construction experience, built the house.

The house is filled with light. Jon had energy-efficient windows specifically positioned to ensure natural ventilation and plenty of "daylighting," a new term for old-fashioned sunlight. The casement windows in the bedrooms, awning win-

OPPOSITE ABOVE The concrete floor, typical of many mid-century houses (though owners often covered the concrete with linoleum or wood parquet tiles), helps to cool the house in the summer and warm it in the winter.

OPPOSITE BELOW All appliances are ENERGY STAR certified. The stainless steel on the backsplash and countertops is recycled. The concrete floors were steel-troweled for smoothness and waxed to a deep shine. True to the period, colors were kept very neutral, except for accents of color here and there.

dows in the living area, and clerestory windows in various rooms of the house were fabricated in vinyl to lower costs and maintenance. Jon selected concrete floors, which absorb the winter sunlight with their thermal mass and gently release it as heat after dark. The efficient heating and cooling system feeds air through ducts run in space (as opposed to through an un-insulated basement or attic), to keep the house comfortable and costing minimal. The house is oriented with the sun so as to receive maximum daylight. The white TPO roof (thermoplastic olefin, a waterproof single-ply roof membrane) reflects solar radiation, which reduces cooling costs during the sticky Dallas summers.

Like Old Friends

The completed house is a thoroughly unique and modern structure that merges perfectly with the mid-century houses in the neighborhood. Designed to be a contemporary version of its neighbors, the house has the lines and angles of the old, but the methods, materials, and energy-efficiency of the new. Jon also wanted the house to be homage to D'Lee's grandfather, who was responsible for building the first houses there decades before.

In the community, Jon and D'Lee's house has sparked a strong interest in the modern ranch style and in green building. Some now ask him to design their new houses, to renovate or add onto existing houses, while others want their version of his house.

Jon believes he succeeded in recreating a classic American house in an energy-efficient, green, and affordable form. He hopes the house will serve not just as a model, but will also "prove that green can be obtainable, affordable, and well designed . . . . [and minimize] our footprint on the earth with smaller homes instead of huge mansions."

BELOW The "fritted" window (a textured glass, providing privacy from the outside) in the shower and the clerestory windows above the mirrors provide natural daylighting, preserving privacy. The vessel sink, wall mounted faucets and metal laminate countertops (low voc adhesive used to attach them) add a contemporary look to this master bathroom.

BOTTOM The clerestory windows in Jon's small office provide much natural light, while leaving room for all the necessary office furnishings.

The large glass doors that open onto the courtyard from Jon's office and dining room extend the living space. In the evening it's a comfortable place for the family to dine and relax. The plants are native and, therefore, require little maintenance.

Believing strongly in yourself and your work is a great thing, though it never hurts to have independent verification of your beliefs. In 2006, the house was selected by the United States Green Building Council as one of the twenty-five greenest structures (of any kind) in North Texas. It was also ranked that year in the top 10 percent of ENERGY STAR Certified Homes in the entire country.

What are SIPs?

Structural Insulated Panels are panels that are manufactured by sandwiching foam insulation between two outer, structural panels of wood (usually oriented strand board or plywood, or even metal). SIPs can be custom designed for a particular house in dimensions as big as 8 x 24 feet. By comparison, standard plywood sheets are 4 x 8 feet. SIPs are increasingly popular for building walls, roofs, floors, and even foundations because of their excellent insulating qualities, strength, short construction time, and low waste. In a house built using SIPs, the heating, ventilation, and air conditioning (HVAC) equipment is scaled down to save money, while the house stays comfortable with lower energy costs. To learn more, visit www.sips.org.

Native Landscaping

Native plants evolved over millennia to adapt to local environments, climates, and moisture conditions. Where water is relatively scarce, landscaping with native plants is called "xeriscaping." Such plants are simple to maintain and often flourish without pesticides, fertilizers, or irrigation. They also provide shelter and food for native wildlife. Planting with native plants also helps improve air quality by reducing the need to mow, which pollutes the air. To learn more go to www. epa.gov/greenacres/nativeplants/factsht.html.

Clerestory Windows

The clerestory windows in Jon's small office provide much natural light, while leaving room for all the necessary office furnishings. Clerestory windows are set in at the top of a wall and can allow a great deal of daylight into the house with only a small amount of heat gain. If these windows open, they can also facilitate cross ventilation in a room where one or more walls might not otherwise have windows. In the winter, south-facing clerestory windows let in the low sunlight for solar gain, while this house's overhangs provide shade from the higher sun in the summer.

A House of Straw

Timber frame/straw bale

PHOTOGRAPHER:

Roger Wade Studio (unless otherwise noted)

ARCHITECT:

Brian Fuentes, Fuentes Design

BUILDER:

Jon Rovick Construction, Inc.

LOCATION:

Leadville, Colorado

SIZE:

2,500 square feet

GREEN ASPECTS:

Straw bale and other local materials

Low VOC

Passive solar

PET carpet

Standing dead trees

Transom windows

Natural finish and pigments

High-efficiency windows

Masonry floor

Radiant heating

Masonry heater

Recycled wood for windowsills

Metal roofing

Ceiling SIPs

ENERGY STAR refrigerator and dishwasher

High-efficiency boiler

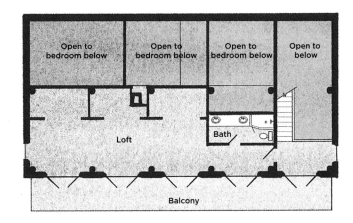

FIRST FLOOR

SECOND FLOOR

LEFT The frame is completed and the straw bales are installed and ready for the plaster to be sprayed on and trowelled to a smooth finish. (Photograph by Jon Rovick)

BELOW The house is protected from the elements with the deep overhangs.

OPPOSITE The piping for the radiant heating system is laid before the final layer of concrete is poured for the floors. (Photograph by Jon Rovick)

M eg and Josh Blum didn't need a second house, but they really wanted one. They wanted a place where they could go hiking, mountain biking, and skiing, a getaway from the hectic world of Denver, with its traffic, work, and manmade environments. Because it would be a luxury and not a necessity, they wanted a second home that took less from the environment, a house that perhaps, in its own way, even gave something back. They wanted a home that would use as little "embodied energy" as possible, and make the least impact on its environment. It would be modestly sized, especially compared to many surrounding homes, which are mammoth, and practically compete with the very Rocky Mountains their owners are there to enjoy. Above all, the house would speak the traditional language of the local built environment.

But how would it be built, and what should it look like?

Searching for a design solution, architect Brian Fuentes reviewed the area's historic structures and hit on an idea that resonated perfectly with the Blums' sensibility: The house would suggest an old mining shack, a structure that conveyed a sense of shelter rather than status.

As Fuentes described it, the Blums wanted "an authentic mountain experience, not a resort mountain experience." It wouldn't look like a resort, "the sort of mountain architecture that is loud and complicated and made to look as if it belongs, instead of [being] something that actually does belong—using local logs, plaster, and craftspeople."

They pushed on. The house would be extraordinarily energy efficient. It would also be built of completely recyclable materials, in adherence to the concept of "cradle-to-cradle." Rather than someday landing in another landfill, its parts could be recycled into another structure in the future. The large timbers they chose for the frame could someday support a new home. The recyclable raw metal roofing could be reformed into some kind of metal creation not yet imagined or even possible. It would be a home with a long view, a home for now and for then.

Working on a Budget

The Blum's house would be all those things as well as a refuge for them and their two children. It would also be affordable.

Being affordable meant making thoughtful choices. It meant using their creativity and having fun making the house their own. For instance, their imagination led them to install open shelving instead of expensive cabinetry. The countertops would be inexpensive granite tile instead of more expensive slabs. They trucked in remnants of "PET" carpet (made from recycled plastic bottles, polyethylene terephthalate) from a home goods store for the children's room and bought their washer and dryer at a local thrift shop. But they splurged where it mattered: on high-efficiency windows and a masonry heater that would help keep the house warm in the cold Colorado winters using as little fuel as possible. And for insulation, the walls would be crafted of 23-inch thick compressed hay bales, generating

OPPOSITE ABOVE The upstairs bunkroom includes a place for the Blum children to play, and for guests to stay over. There are two niches in the house, one of which is in this room, which can store small art objects or work as a built-in bookcase.

OPPOSITE BELOW Open shelving reduced the amount of wood needed to outfit the kitchen with storage. Brackets (by Rovick) give a natural and rustic appearance to the cabinetry.

OVERLEAF Positioned in the center of the great room, the masonry heater quietly radiates warmth and comfort that reaches throughout the densely insulated house. Massive timbers offer reassurance of strength. The concrete floor provides dense thermal mass, which absorbs heat and gently radiates it even when the heating is turned off.

Straw Bale Construction

Settlers on the Great Plains built their homes with straw bale because that's what they had. But once the railroad made timber and brick affordable, straw dropped out of favor. Yet a testament to straw bale's unyielding strength as a building material is the continued existence of one-hundred-year-old straw bale houses in the Midwest. And in the past thirty years, energy concerns have revived straw-bale construction—and for good reason. Straw is excellent insulation and makes use of a material that has generally been considered best burned in the fields after the wheat, rye, or oats have been harvested. As added benefits, straw is inexpensive and its density keeps a house comfortable year-round. It's also superb for sound insulation. If you're interested in building with straw, check with your building inspector and mortgage lender to see if they allow it.

Masonry Heaters

Masonry heaters work best in a well-insulated house like the Blums', where the heavy mass of the stove and floor retain heat and radiate it for hours after the fire is out. The Blums' masonry heater was strategically placed at the center of the downstairs living space to warm the whole house. The straw insulation holds in the heat, while the concrete floors absorb it and slowly emit warmth throughout the night. This is how masonry heaters work: A fire within heats the dense mass of the heater, which stores and gently radiates its heat throughout the space, warming the room for hours after the initial fire is extinguished. Compare that to a standard fireplace, which has a roaring blaze that is too hot to get very close to, and burns out soon thereafter. Also, masonry heaters emit less pollution because of their efficiency.

insulation values anywhere from R-43 to as high as R-70 (an average 6-inch thick wall filled with fiberglass insulation has a value of R-19 to R-21). The natural insulation would keep their home incredibly warm. The heavy timbers—crafted like giant furniture into a timber frame—would keep their home incredibly strong.

Passive Aggressive

It might seem as if creating a house that used a tiny amount of energy to operate and could be recycled in the future would be green enough. But the Blums wanted to squeeze out more efficiency. That search brought them to passive solar. They had the house oriented so as to absorb the maximum amount of the low-hanging sun's energy during the coldest months. Large overhangs would keep the higher summer sun out of the windows and shelter the house from the elements throughout the year.

Transom windows, which are generally used above windows and doors, were used in a nontraditional way in the Blum house. Brian decided to position them on the upper portion of the bedroom walls, so that the light from the sunniest rooms also illuminates rear spaces that receive less light. The transom windows add to the "daylighting" in the rooms, while also providing privacy and reducing the need for energy required for lighting.

Brian left concrete floors bare in most areas of the house. Several pigments were mixed together, creating a surface with irregular, brown tones. With a high thermal mass, the concrete floors store and slowly release or reradiate large quantities of heat, helping to keep the house warm. In the colder months, heat from the sun comes in through the windows and is absorbed by the concrete during the day; when the sun goes down, that heat can be released

several hours later. Concrete floors, along with the masonry heater, and deep overhangs, contribute to the house's passive solar energy, limiting the need for mechanical heat and excessive fuel.

Reducing Embodied Energy

Once the Blums and Brian got the design down and began choosing the materials, they were on a roll. The straw bale came from a neighboring farm. The timbers used to support the walls and roof were harvested locally. The plaster over the straw bale walls was installed by Anikke Storm, a local craftswoman who camped on the property with her crew while they plastered the house inside and out in about a week. The plaster was a mix of local clay, sand, and wheat paste, and the pigments were all natural and found nearby.

The brackets that support the kitchen shelving are made of twisted piñon branches that were painstakingly scribed, or fitted together. The outside balusters on the handrail were crafted from

simple rebar (concrete reinforcement), an inexpensive material.

The Strength of Straw

When they began searching for the log timbers for their home, the Blums found they could harvest dead trees from a burnt forest. To preserve the natural beauty of the burnt logs, they removed the bark to expose the rich patina of the fire-hardened wood. The logs were flattened on one side to fit flush against the straw bales. Then they were prefabricated into the frame at a local Breckenridge building yard, labeled, shipped to the site, and fitted together on the foundation.

Finally, once the straw bales were in place, the plaster finish was applied inside and out. Unlike concrete, which seals walls and prevents them from "breathing," clay plaster allows moisture to escape from the straw, keeping it dry, and increasing the longevity of the structure. The natural plaster also doesn't give off gas fumes the way some painted finishes would.

Tall + Narrow House

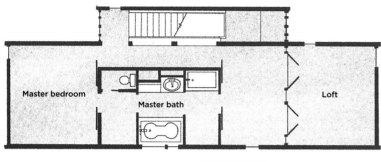

SECOND FLOOR

Master bedroom

Master bath

Loft

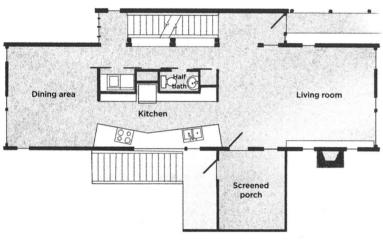

FIRST FLOOR

Dining area

Kitchen

Half Bath

Living room

Screened porch

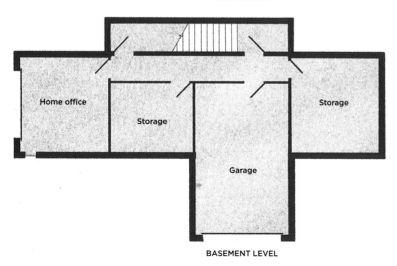

BASEMENT LEVEL

Home office

Storage

Storage

Garage

Panelized

PHOTOGRAPHERS:

Charles Register, interiors; Eric Roth, exteriors;
Randall Lanou, construction photos

DESIGNER/BUILDER:

Randall Lanou, BuildSense, Inc.

LOCATION:

Durham, North Carolina

SIZE:

2,000 square feet

RATINGS:

Green Building Initiative

GREEN ASPECTS:

High-efficiency HVAC system

High-efficiency windows and doors

Spray foam insulation

Tankless water heater

Passive solar design

Small lot

Urban infill lot

Low-flow faucets

Renewable resources

Precast concrete foundation

ENERGY STAR appliances

Bamboo flooring

OPPOSITE Three sustainable, durable materials were used for the siding: Atlantic white cedar, cementitious panels, and Galvalume metal. The large overhang prevents the summer sun from warming the house, while admitting light from the low winter sun. (Photo by Eric Roth)

David Shamlin loved the neighborhood of Durham, North Carolina, but he could not find the right house. The neighborhood rarely sees turnover, and when one of the older houses come on the market, they often need renovation, something that can be trickier, costlier, and more problematic than all-new construction.

Nevertheless, David decided it would be cheaper to remodel one of these houses than to build a brand new one. But as luck would have it, one of the area's last empty lots came on the market at just the right time. It was an incredibly small infill lot (2/10 of an acre), but big enough to build the type of house he needed.

The Right Architect

After searching for a local designer whose design sense matched his own, David found Randy Lanou of BuildSense, Inc. They immediately clicked, and David left that first encounter with confidence that Randy could design and build the house he wanted.

Randy's company appeared to be very quality conscious, which was important to David. And Randy shared David's vision of the house, which would have very strong lines, an industrial flavor to the exterior, and a surprisingly comfortable and warm character to the interior. Bamboo flooring, cherry wood, and natural colors throughout the interior would create an inviting, livable environment.

It's difficult to say "where his ideas stopped and mine started," David recalled. They collaborated to come up with the final design. Randy suggested open shelving on the staircase to use what would otherwise be wasted space. David came up with the idea of using metal sheeting to wrap the mantel shelf.

Maximum Energy Efficient

BuildSense both designed and fabricated the panels for the exterior walls of the house. Five and a half inches of insulation make the walls incredibly tight and energy efficient. Add to that energy-efficient windows and doors and a precast, insulated, concrete basement, and you see that David got a house that's heavy on energy conservation, low on energy costs, and visually striking.

To take advantage of the warming power of the sun, the house was designed with a large awning in the front, so that in winter, when the sun is low, the windows catch the sun's rays. In summer, the awning blocks the high sun, and keeps the house cooler. David says his electric bills—for cooling, heating, and everything else—have never topped 100 dollars a month. To supplement the passive solar energy, David had a high-velocity HVAC system installed. He added a screened porch to make a comfortable area where he could "sit with a newspaper and a cup of coffee in the morning."

Other measures were taken to make the house more efficient. David chose a tankless water heater (see Tankless or On-Demand Hot Water sidebar, page 102)—which he has never

OPPOSITE ABOVE Spray-in-place foam insulation. (Photo by Randall Lanou)

OPPOSITE BELOW David left the balcony open to the lower floor, but says it can be closed with pivoting doors providing privacy for future owners. (Photo by Charles Kegister)

Spray Foam Insulation

There are very good reasons why spray foam insulation has become so popular. When applied inside exterior walls, "open cell" foam insulation expands up to 150 times its original volume in seconds, blocking air leaks and insulating like few other materials could. Insulation this thorough improves air quality and reduces noise. Icynene is a patented brand and a company that pioneered open-cell spray insulation. When used in place of traditional fiberglass, Icynene can reduce heating and cooling costs by up to 50 percent, and in so doing, deliver a corresponding reduction in the home's greenhouse gas emissions. Its climate-friendly formulation is also free of HFCs (Hydro-fluorocarbons), which are blowing agents that the EPA has deemed high on the list of potential global warming agents. Demilac, another open-cell insulation, was used on this house. The insulation remains flexible after applied, so it won't crack or start leaking air during the natural expansion and contraction of the wood frame. New open-cell products, such as BioBased Insulation, include a bio-based product that contains soybean oil.

An older alternative is closed-cell spray insulation, which is more costly, less flexible than open-cell foam (giving it the potential to crack and compromise the air barrier) but has a higher R-value. It does not, however, absorb water as open-cell foam may if it's inadequately protected. To learn more, visit www.icynene.com, www.demilecusa.com, www.biobased.net, and www.certain teed.com.

LEFT Bookshelves line the side of the staircase, making best use of space, and creating an interesting design texture. The open stairs provide light and an airiness to the center of the house. (Photo by Charles Register)

OPPOSITE ABOVE The cherry wood kitchen cabinets were made locally. Flooring throughout the house is made of bamboo. Appliances are ENERGY STAR rated, which helps lower the electricity bill. Windows and exterior doors are vinyl-clad and require only occasional cleanings. Both location and shape of the windows provide maximum privacy, views, and ventilation. (Photo by Charles Register)

OPPOSITE BELOW The windows in the living area were set just so to provide the best possible mixture of light and privacy. The fireplace is flush with the wall for a clean, contemporary look. On the outside, it bumps out to add an interesting design element. The exterior metal smokestack complements the home's clean, contemporary design. (Photo by Charles Register)

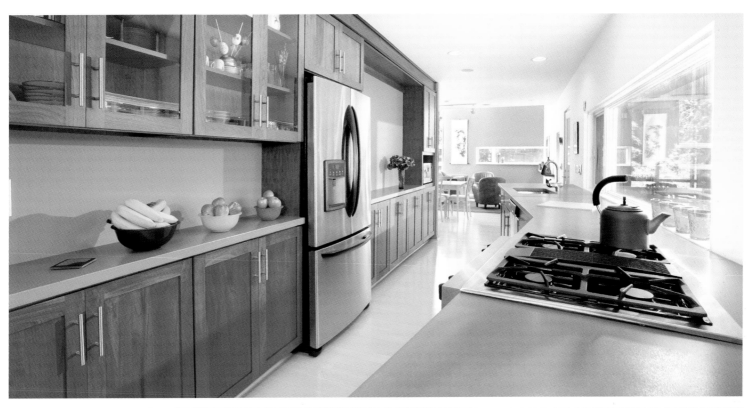

What Is Panelized Construction?

One of the most common forms of prefabrication, panelized construction uses interior and exterior wall sections, as well as floor and roof sections which are built in a factory and shipped to the building site to be erected. Some panels come with windows and doors installed; others come with openings only. Many factories now build panels using computer-guided machinery, which cuts the wood to exact blueprint specifications. This kind of precision means less waste, and a tighter and stronger house. Using panels built in a climate-controlled facility, allows you to avoid warping, mold, and other damage caused by weather. The panels also take less time to raise, which reduces on-site construction costs and speeds up construction-time from weeks or months to days. Panelization saves materials, on-site clean-up, and time. To learn more, visit www.nahb.org.

Precast Insulated Concrete Foundations

The concrete panels that comprise the foundation on this house were produced in a factory with a concrete mix that contains polystyrene insulation and steel reinforcement bars (rebar). Walls are poured with openings for windows and doors, as well as wiring access and wood or metal furring strips for attaching drywall or paneling. Installation is significantly faster than that for poured foundations, and sometimes takes as little as a day. Curing of the concrete is unnecessary because it is cured in the factory. A precast foundation may be more expensive than a typical poured foundation, but there's potential future savings on energy costs and labor to prepare the basement walls for finishing. There is also superior durability. The concrete's high density (5,000 psi), and the moisture resistance of the foam form a system that is a strong barrier against moisture and the transfer of heat and cold. Because the walls are factory poured, waste is minimal and there's much less impact on the building site (i.e., heavy concrete trucks can crush tree roots). To learn more, visit the National Precast Concrete Association at www.precast.org.

OPPOSITE The basement level includes a garage, storage space, and a home office. (Photo by Eric Roth)

ABOVE A screened porch over the garage is a wonderful place to relax in the fresh air. The horizontal slats on the structure are both a design and a privacy feature. The wood is locally harvested Atlantic White Cedar, which is insect-resistant and very durable. (Photo by Charles Register)

regretted—although it takes three to five years for the system to pay for itself. But he has hot water whenever he needs it, and the shower, dishwasher, and washing machine can all run at the same time with only this one unit.

David wanted the exterior to need as little maintenance as possible, to conserve time, resources, and money. So he and Randy chose three very durable and sustainable products for the siding, all of which are low maintenance, sustainable, and give the house a clean, beauti-ful appearance. They went with locally harvested Atlantic White Cedar, a very durable material, and a cementitious panel siding, Cembonit, also known for its durability. The third material, Galval-ume, similar to what people use for barn siding, is a mixture of zinc and aluminum that helps protect steel from corroding. David says the color of the metal seems to change with the weather: Sometimes it's blue reflecting the color of the sky, other times it's green, or gray, or just a glowing silver.

Eastbourne House

Steel frame

PHOTOGRAPHER:

Stacey Brandford Photography Inc.

ARCHITECT:

Boyd Montgomery, Watchorn Architect Inc.

BUILDER:

Fifthshire Homes Limited

FRAME MANUFACTURER:

Bailey Metal Products

LOCATION:

Georgina, Ontario

SIZE:

3,423 square feet

RATINGS:

R-2000 EnviroHome

GREEN ASPECTS:

Galvanized light gauge steel frame

Heat recovery ventilator

High-efficiency vinyl windows (low-E, argon gas
    with warm-edge spacers)

On-demand hot water heater and space heating

CFLs and halogen lights

Low-flush toilets

ENERGY STAR appliances

ENERGY STAR ceiling fans

Low-flow faucets and showerheads

Spray foam insulation

Native planting

Composite trellis

Low-VOC paints and varnishes

Low-emission composite cabinetry

Natural cedar decking

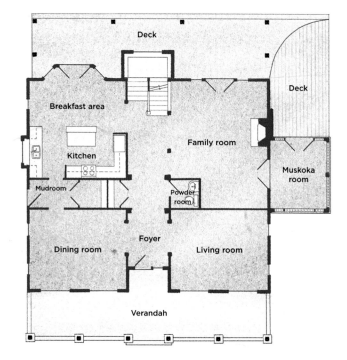

FIRST FLOOR

SECOND FLOOR

Canada is simply much colder than the United States, which helps explain why during the energy crisis of the 1970s, Canadians felt a greater urgency to improve their understanding of energy-efficient building.

The result of their research is a concept called "the house as a system," which was to energy efficiency what the microprocessor was to computer technology: a big conceptual revelation that changed things forever. By understanding the house as one big system made up of many smaller, interconnected systems, builders began to understand how one poorly built part affected the whole construction. The result: Houses would be greener and more energy efficient.

It's no exaggeration to say that this thinking changed the way builders and architects around the world approached design and construction. All modern building science is based on the "house as a system" concept. So to spread the word to builders, the Canadian government launched its energy-efficient and healthy home construction program, called R-2000. When the program began, custom builders Fifthshire Homes had been building houses for fifteen years.

A Higher Standard

Fifthshire's owners Joe Vella and his brother-in-law and partner, John DeCarlo, took a course in R-2000 and immediately began building their homes to the standards. Inspired by their new understanding, and by a desire to provide cutting-edge quality to their customers, Fifthshire first demonstrated their commitment to the program by switching from wood-frame to light steel-frame construction. The quality of the lumber they used had been declining and often arrived at the construction site bowed or twisted, which made it difficult to build straight, flat walls. Also, they were getting more and more service calls because of "nail pops," the lump you see in drywall when a screw or nail pulls loose from the wood frame. Drywall fastened to a steel frame never has this problem. Fifthshire decided to resolve these problems by building their homes with steel frames.

The steel-framed Eastbourne House was built as a model for a development on Ontario's Lake Simcoe. Although the U.S. Environmental Protection Agency's ENERGY STAR program has become more widely adopted as an energy-rating system in Canada, Fifthshire Homes continues to build their homes to the higher standards of Canada's R-2000 system. For their efforts, they produce a more energy-efficient house.

Because of the steel framing, which is made from recycled material, and the other green systems they added to the house (such as spray foam insulation, water-saving fixtures, and low VOC paints), the Eastbourne House was chosen as one of Canada's ten EnviroHome houses in 2008 (See What's an EnviroHome? sidebar, page 85).

Muskoka rooms, inspired by the picturesque lake district of Ontario, are sunrooms typically with windows on three sides to draw in an abundance of light. They also provide plenty of room for seating, so the whole family and friends can enjoy the room's lush exposure to the outdoors. Like many Muskoka rooms, this one is well insulated so it can be used all year long.

LEFT The coffered celing in the dining room adds an elegant touch to this traditionally designed home.

RIGHT The appliances are ENERGY STAR rated, and the cabinets are made from composite wood, which does not off-gas (off-gassing occurs when building materials release chemicals into the air through evaporation).

All ceiling fans, including this one in the living room, are ENERGY STAR rated. The fireplace is a direct-vent gas model, which requires no chimney, and is more energy efficient than a wood-burning fireplace, which loses much of its heat up the chimney.

What's an EnviroHome?

EnviroHome is a designation given by the Canadian Home Builders' Association (CHBA) to a maximum of ten houses a year. To be selected, a house must have been certified to the R-2000 Standard, include additional air quality and environmental features beyond the R-2000 Program, and get certification by a third-party inspection to ensure the highest level of energy efficiency. The EnviroHome program was established in 1994 by CHBA and TD Canada Trust as a marketing initiative to recognize and support innovative builders who build houses that are better for the environment, healthier for inhabitants, affordable, comfortable, and energy efficient.

Heat and Energy Recovery Ventilation Systems

In the past, houses were not sealed or well insulated, so fresh air was never a problem; it simply flowed in and out through walls and roofs. However, in a contemporary, highly insulated, and tightly sealed house, a mechanical ventilation system that exhausts stale air and brings in fresh air is a necessity. To avoid wasting heating or cooling, new ventilation systems pre-heat or pre-cool incoming fresh air by extracting the warmth or coolness of outgoing air, which is known as heat or energy recovery. Heat recovery ventilators, or HRVs, are recommended for colder and dryer areas. Energy recovery ventilators, or ERVs, exhaust water vapor and are recommended for warm, humid climates. To learn more, go to www.eere.energy.gov.

The Frame of Steel

Fifthshire Homes uses steel framing for floors, walls, ceilings, and roofs because steel doesn't shrink, warp, and twist like wood. Steel also contains more than eighty percent recycled content, and steel can itself be recycled or reused. The steel frame is cut to exact measurements in the factory, eliminating the waste of on-site wood-frame construction. Steel is also stronger than wood, and can span larger spaces without the need for load-bearing walls in between. The entire metal cavity of the steel framing in the Eastbourne house was filled with spray foam insulation, eliminating gaps or spaces that could reduce energy efficiency.

2

GREENER HOUSES

It's important to discuss climate change and the overarching issues we need to address as members of our global community. Yet, the first step is addressing these issues on a smaller scale—our homes are a good place to start.

Homeowners are beginning to understand how thinking green and acting green can positively affect our lives. We know that wastefulness and inefficiency harm the environment. Now we need to act on that knowledge. Few things are more wasteful and inefficient than new home construction. Fortunately, more and more homeowners are becoming committed to conserving energy in their homes, using sustainable materials and limiting the environmental impact of their homes. The sooner we create healthier environments, the better our lives will be. The homes in this book are healthier homes, without the VOCs, mold, and countless other biological and chemical pollutants.

Homeowners are also learning the financial advantages of green, which include lower utility costs, tax incentives and rebates, and lower maintenance and replacement costs. And thanks to this growing awareness, there is an understanding that green houses have greater worth per square foot than non-green houses. When the owners of a green house decide to sell, they're going to get a better price than their non-green neighbors. Local and state governments are going to enact ever more strict green and energy-efficient standards. As that happens, even more people will embrace the value of green.

The common misconception is that green is too expensive and only for the wealthy. This argument is beginning to lose traction. While a home built with the latest green techniques and technologies may cost somewhat more upfront, the added cost is negligible compared to the investment.

Think of it this way: Would you rather spend a bit more to get a car with high fuel efficiency, or instead save some money up front on a cheaper car that gets terrible mileage, wastes energy, and you'll be stuck with for years? It's definitely worth paying a bit more upfront for sustainability and savings in the long run.

As the popularity of the green movement grows, production of green products will increase and prices will drop. Competition is growing among manufacturers to produce these products, which will bring down cost. However, many green construction options cost very little, or sometimes nothing. A properly oriented house with properly placed windows will make maximum use of the sun's energy (referred to as "passive solar"). You'll find daylighting and passive solar techniques in almost every house in this book. Concrete floors create a thermal mass that absorbs that sunlight to keep the house warm in winter. If the windows are correctly positioned, that concrete floor stays out of the sun in summer and cool throughout the day.

Modular construction, as seen in the Glen Cairn Cottage, The Method Cabin, The Wave Cottage and EcoFabulous House, is built under optimal conditions—protected from the elements, sparing of material,

conscious of efficiency and waste. Many factories now return leftover materials to manufacturers for recycling, or use waste for other purposes—such as heating the factory itself, or for manufacturing engineered wood products.

The same is true of panelized companies, such as the prefabricator that built the Rebecca Leland Farmhouse, a place where skilled workers build homes in a controlled environment, under supervision. Houses such as Farmhouse Bungalow and The Porretto House were built with SIPs, which have quick installation times, high R-values, continuous insulation, and help keep noise out and energy in. Designers of The Palms House house embraced several of the best construction technologies available, including modular building, SIPs, and steel construction, creating not only a beautiful house, but one that is durable, energy efficient, and sustainable.

As is demonstrated by many of the houses in this book, you don't have to sacrifice luxury to go green. In fact, luxury is enhanced by adding energy efficiency and sustainability to the house description. Being green has become politically correct and an increasingly respected way of life.

The Porretto House

Timber frame/SIPs

PHOTOGRAPHERS:

Susan Sully (unless otherwise noted)

MANUFACTURER:

Riverbend Timber Framing; Insulspan

ARCHITECT:

Roger Rasbach, Fred Pecceni

BUILDER:

SBS Sustainable Building Solutions, Inc.

LOCATION:

Dewees Island, South Carolina

SIZE:

3,000 square feet

GREEN ASPECTS:

Untreated, reclaimed wood

Mold-resistant, paper-free wallboard

Nontoxic plaster wall surfaces

Closed loop geothermal HVAC system

Tankless water heaters

ENERGY STAR appliances

CFLs

Eco-friendly, disaster-resistant, slate-like composite roof tiles

High-efficiency, impact-resistant windows

Paperless drywall

Natural plaster

Sustainably harvested cypress siding and porches

High-efficiency plumbing system

Rainwater harvesting

Graywater system

Tongue and groove subfloor for extra support

Spray foam insulation

FIRST FLOOR

SECOND FLOOR

OPPOSITE Built on reinforced pilings that keep it anchored and secure from flooding, the house is a structural marvel. To keep the place maintenance free, cypress siding, which is naturally weathered and insect resistant, was left unstained to weather to a natural gray.

John and Sue Anne Porretto never knew retirement would be so much work.

When John, a former health care CEO retired, the plan was to build a second home on South Carolina's Dewees Island. The couple wanted to build a house that would exceed local codes in structure, energy efficiency, safety, and indoor air quality. They wanted their home to fit naturally into the lovely coastal environment, not compete with it.

When John and Sue discovered Dewee's Island—an environmentally conscious, little island community off the Carolina coast—they fell in love with it. Working first with the late Roger Rasbach, an architect known for his energy-efficient designs, John began interviewing local contractors. All of the builders were "competing on price rather than quality," he said, which went against his CEO grain. Unwilling to go the lowest-bid route, he decided to build the house himself. Rasbach essentially completed the drawings for the house, though after he died, architect Fred Pecceni added some finishing touches. In 2005, John established his new company, Sustainable Building Solutions (SBS), and began construction.

Building on the Coast

No matter how beautiful, a coastal environment is harsh. Wind, salt water, year-round humidity, and the chance of a devastating hurricane are just some of the challenges. John took every precaution to ensure the house could survive the hurricanes and high winds that sooner or later will strike. Whatever was required to secure the house to its site, John took it a few steps further.

Working with architects, he oversaw design of the engineered foundation. Raised high above the potential storm surge, the house sits on thick wood posts that are cross-braced and fastened with heavy steel fittings. The timbers plug into heavy concrete beams in the ground (called "grade beams"). And all that is further anchored by mammoth steel helical piles, which are like gargantuan woodscrews, literally pinning the house to the earth. The house is designed to survive the harshest winds, tidal waves, and earthquakes.

Sitting on top of this impressive foundation is the timber frame. Both sturdy and strong, the frame is made even more substantial by its highly insulated skin of SIPs. The first level of the structure is open, so water can rush through without hitting the house and demolishing it. John insulated beneath the house with 6 inches of Icynene foam, (see Spray Foam Insulation sidebar, page 75) which he covered with wood. The roof is composed of synthetic slate. Structurally strong and environmentally friendly, the tiles are made from recycled rubber and can endure hail and winds up to 130 miles per hour.

A Comfortable Interior

The house is oriented so as to catch the breezes off the ocean, and to be lit as much as possible by the light of the sun. The expansive windows are impact-resistant, and tilt and turn to direct air flow. Both the windows and doors are engineered

OPPOSITE The master bedroom on the second floor is light and airy as a result of the glass-filled doors, high ceilings, large windows, and ceiling fan. The beautiful artwork, collected by the owners, adds a warm and colorful touch to the natural surroundings.

to withstand 145 mile-per-hour winds. All the materials John chose for the interior of the house are natural products that don't off-gas, keeping indoor air pure and healthful. The plaster finish (see Natural Plaster sidebar, opposite) inside is made from clay and pigments found in nature. No composite board, toxic glues, or any other product that would off-gas was used in the construction. All the interior surfaces require minimal upkeep and maintenance.

A geothermal heat pump (see Geothermal Heat Pumps sidebar, opposite) keeps the house warm in the winter and cool in the summer. To take off the chill and stoke up the mood, John had a masonry fireplace installed in the living room. The fireplace is efficient, modular, and doesn't require a heavy masonry foundation. He wanted the house to use as little energy as possible, and because the SIPs make the house virtually airtight, the need for mechanical heating and cooling is minimal. ENERGY STAR appliances further reduce energy use. The couple's average utility bill is $83 a month.

After completing his home, John's new contracting company began building houses for other people interested in having their own sustainable, long-lasting, and energy-efficient homes built. Using the same high standards and quality he put into his own home and the commercial projects he oversaw during his career, he now puts into every home he builds for others.

BELOW The prefabricated timber frame is in place before the SIPs are installed. (Photo by John Porretto)

BOTTOM The view from the rear of the house of the marsh and intra-coastal canal. Dewee's Island is the first major environmentally conscious island in the southeast. The community is committed to sustainability and to preserving the natural beauty of its barrier island ecosystem

The SIPs panels are lifted into place and attached to the timber frame.
(Photo by John Porretto)

Paperless Drywall

Paper-faced drywall (or gypsum board) doesn't take well to water. If this type of drywall gets damp, it tends to grow moldy, or falls apart. For high humidity areas, paperless drywall is a dream come true. After talking with a distributor who had tested the product in post-Katrina New Orleans, John decided to give the paperless version a try. Though it's a bit more expensive than typical drywall, the paperless drywall has thus far lived up to its reputation.

Geothermal Heat Pumps

Geothermal systems use the earth's constant temperature to maintain that same steady temperature in the home. The technology can supply heating, cooling, and water heating, and it can be used with a conventional duct system or a radiant floor system. To install geothermal heat pumps, workers lay pipes in the ground (either horizontally or vertically) in holes drilled down to approximately 400 feet, depending on the site and the home-owner's needs. Open-loop systems use well water as an energy source. The system can cost 50–100 percent more to install than typical HVAC systems, though homeowners definitely end up saving money on heating and cooling costs. Some electric utilities offer incentives for investing in a GHP system. To learn more, visit www.eere.energy.gov or www.toolbase.org.

Natural Plaster

John chose American Clay plaster, an environmentally friendly alternative to cement, gypsum, acrylic, or lime plaster. American Clay plaster contains natural clay, recycled and reclaimed aggregates, and natural pigment. Also, there's little waste with this product, because the excess can be broken up, mixed with water, and then reused. The plaster can be sprayed or troweled on like traditional plaster. Because the plaster "breathes" with changes in humidity, it won't crack. Additionally, if there are any damages they can easily be repaired. This nontoxic material doesn't attract dust. John used the clay plaster throughout the house because of its practicality and natural look, which is consistent with the design of his house. Of all the green products he discovered in his home-building odyssey, this was John's favorite.

The warmth of the timber frame and plaster walls are enhanced with maple cabinets that have seeded glass insets. Recycled heart pine flooring casts a rich amber glow.

LEFT Many of the natural elements of this house are on display in the gathering room: a pumice-stone fireplace, plaster walls, reclaimed heart pine flooring, and the beautiful exposed timbers of the frame. Above the fireplace, the number "2005" was burned into the frame to commemorate the year the house was built. Such dating is traditional practice among timber framers.

RIGHT The master bathroom.

The Palms House

Modular/SIPs/Steel

PHOTOGRAPHER:

David Lena (unless otherwise noted)

ARCHITECT:

Ron Radziner, FAIA; Leo Marmol, FAIA

MANUFACTURER & BUILDER:

Marmol Radziner Prefab

LOCATION:

Venice, California

SIZE:

2,800 square feet

GREEN ASPECTS:

Passive ventilation

Solar orientation

Recycled steel

Recycled denim insulation

PV panels

Radiant heating

FSC certified wood

CFL lighting

Cabinets made from formaldehyde-free MDF board

Recycled steel frame

Natural cotton fiber insulation

High-efficiency glass

FSC-certified EcoTimber flooring

On-demand tankless water heater

Low VOC paint

Instant tankless water heater

ENERGY STAR appliances

ENERGY STAR-rated HVAC system

Expansive deck spaces

Composite (recycled content) counters

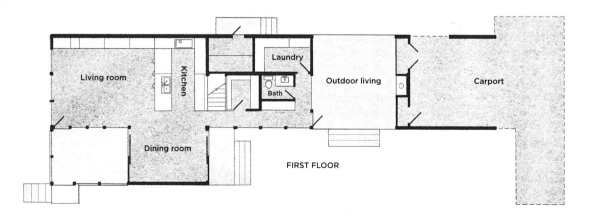

SECOND FLOOR

Master bedroom • Master bathroom • Bedroom • Bedroom • Office • Outdoor living

FIRST FLOOR

Living room • Kitchen • Laundry • Bath • Outdoor living • Carport • Dining room

OPPOSITE Cedar siding looks great and is highly weather and insect resistant, making it an extremely sustainable feature of this house. The heavy lattice wall provides privacy while allowing light and air into the space. The enclosed courtyard connects the interior with the exterior.

Venice is one of California's most interesting and eclectic beach towns, which is why Leo Marmol and his family love living there. The only problem in Venice is space. Where the Marmols lived, there wasn't enough of it, and Leo, his wife, and daughter needed more.

The best property the family could find for a new house in popular Venice was a 40-foot-wide infill lot, not the kind of space they were hoping for. But thanks to the fact that Leo's firm owns a modular house factory, in a short three months, Leo's company built his new house, delivered it, and in two and a half days, it was set.

With about six weeks of on-site finishing work, the house was complete. It served as a show home for a few months, and then the Marmols moved into their beautiful new home. The narrow lot was a challenge because Leo wanted his house to have some usable outdoor space. To create an open yard, the house was designed to be just 20 feet wide (a combination of 12-foot and 8-foot modules). The modules, or "boxes," were set on the north side of the property to allow for a side yard along the south side of the house.

A Prefab Company is Born

Leo and his partner, Ron Radziner, have been designing and building houses together since 1989. But growing concerns over weather delays, material delays, and tardy or no-show subcontractors forced them to rethink their business. Step by step, they found themselves fabricating more of their houses in their own shop. Prefab intrigued them. After years of watching waste pile up, energy consumed, and construction delayed at their site-built houses, they set up their own fabrication factory in 2006. Prefabrication gave Leo and Ron greater control over the building process, ensured a higher level of quality, and allowed them to actually set a schedule and keep it by minimizing the parts of the process beyond their control.

They chose to build their modular houses with steel frames and structural insulated panels. They elected to use steel because it's "the best solution for modern modular construction . . . [and] allows for long clear spans of space, which allows the house to feel more open and flow out to the outdoors." The houses Leo and Ron design have frames made of strong, recyclable steel, which form the perimeter structure of the modules and SIPs forming the floors, walls, and roof that span between the steel. Floors, walls, and roof are all in place and insulated in one step.

Unlike normal home construction materials, SIPs are factory-made, maximizing material efficiency while minimizing waste. When they're delivered to the Marmol Radziner Prefab factory, they're ready to install. Each panel contains airtight, draft-free insulation and moisture barriers, which come together to ensure that houses are much tighter and more energy efficient than standard construction. With such effective insulation, these houses require much less energy to cool or heat than ordinary houses. Prefab homes

OPPOSITE Roughly 700 square feet of deck provides lots of options for outdoor enjoyment. Overhangs shade the walls and reduce solar gain in the summer. Wide doors open to the outside allow natural cross ventilation. All the landscaping was designed for native plants, which require minimal maintenance.

TOP 90 percent of the house was completed in the factory, including built-ins, flooring, and kitchen cabinets. Even the wood siding was installed in the factory, unlike most modular construction, in which the siding is installed on-site. (Photo supplied by Marmol Radziner + Associates)

CENTER A flatbed truck makes the trip from the factory to the building site in Venice. (Photo supplied by Marmol Radziner + Associates)

BOTTOM A section is lifted into place for the second floor. (Photo supplied by Marmol Radziner + Associates)

LEFT All appliances are ENERGY STAR rated. The walnut-veneer cabinets were made in Leo and Ron's factory using formaldehyde-free cores. High windows provide light and privacy, while the big skylight both brings in light and opens for added ventilation.

BELOW The furnishings in this light filled room were built in their factory.

What FSC Is All About

The non-profit Forest Stewardship Council encourages the responsible management of the world's forests. FSC's accredited and independent third-party certifiers assess forest management to ensure environmentally responsible practices. They also track forest products (chain-of-custody certification, or COC) to identify those trees from a certified source. Products that bear the FSC logo are guaranteed to be derived from wood that comes from well managed forests. Control of this sort leads to less deforestation of the world's old growth forests. FSC products are available at major retailers around the country. For further information, or to find retailers in your area, check www.fscus.org.

Tankless or On-Demand Hot Water

On-demand water heaters live up to their name—they provide hot water only when you want it. That means you're not wasting energy heating water when you don't need it. In on-demand water heaters, cold water circulates through a series of coils, which are directly heated by gas burners or electric coils. The unit only kicks on when you turn on the hot water faucet. On-demand water heaters provide hot water at a rate of 2 to 5 gallons per minute, depending on the model. Gas-fired on-demand water heaters produce higher flow rates than the electric ones. You might need a second unit if your family's hot water demands are great. Some units provide enough hot water only for a tub or washing machine at one time; others can supply enough for multiple simultaneous needs. These generally cost more than a typical 40-gallon water heater, but usually have longer warranties, last longer, and allow you to save money on energy. To learn more, visit the Department of Energy Efficiency and Renewable Energy web site at www.eere.energy.gov.

BELOW The high windows in the master bathroom provide light and privacy. The countertops are recycled quartz.

BOTTOM Except for upholstered pieces (which the firm designed but someone else built), all furniture was built in their factory. The custom walnut casework in the living room and kitchen was built and installed in the factory.

All of the cabinetry and beds in the house, including those in the Marmols' daughter's room, were custom built in the factory from FSC-certified walnut.

consume nearly 15 percent less energy than typical houses.

Unlike most companies that produce prefabricated houses, Leo and Ron also make many of the built-ins for their houses, including cabinets and platform beds, floorings, and other types of millwork. When one of their houses is delivered, it's about 90 percent complete.

Green and Natural

Although the house has a lot of green features, Leo decided against getting green certification. Their production schedule was tight from the start, and waiting for LEED certification would have disrupted the process. But being green and energy efficient without certification brings the same ultimate reward. Factory construction minimized waste and allowed for recycling. It also dramatically reduced noise, dust, damage to the landscape, and disruption in the neighborhood.

To ensure that the wood used in the structure was responsibly harvested, Leo chose FSC-certified lumber (see What FSC Is All About sidebar, opposite). ENERGY STAR appliances limit the

home's energy consumption, and a highly efficient gas furnace reduces utilities by 30 percent. The "on-demand" tankless water heater (see Tankless or On-Demand Hot Water sidebar, opposite) conserves up to 20 percent more energy than a conventional water heater. Radiant heat keeps the family comfortable on cool days, thanks to the thermal mass advantage of the concrete floor.

The architects used several techniques to provide natural light, ventilation, and privacy for the family in such a close environment. Windows high up on the walls of the kitchen and bathrooms, louvers on other windows, native landscaping, and artfully placed fencing all enhanced the quality of the house.

Large expanses of high-efficiency glass on the south side of the house flood the house with light and warmth. In the cooler months, the dense concrete floors absorb the sun's heat during the day and release it in the evening to gently warm the house. In the summer, the concrete floors help keep the house cool.

Rebecca Leland Farmhouse

Panelized

PHOTOGRAPHER:

Jim Westphalen (unless otherwise noted)

MANUFACTURER & DESIGNER:

Connor Homes

BUILDER:

Columbia County Historic Homes

LOCATION:

Chatham, New York

SIZE:

3,258 square feet

RATINGS:

ENERGY STAR

GREEN ASPECTS:

Photovoltaic solar system

Passive solar design

Solar hot water

Radiant floors

High-efficiency windows

No-VOC paints

ICF foundation

Reclaimed light fixtures

Reclaimed wood floors

Low-flush toilets

Spray foam insulation

Energy-efficient appliances

High-efficiency boiler

Energy recovery ventilator (ERV)

Reclaimed landscaping stones

Standing seam metal roof

Linoleum flooring

Cork flooring

Locally harvested cherry wood for cabinets, shelving, and paneling

Environmentally sensitive landscaping

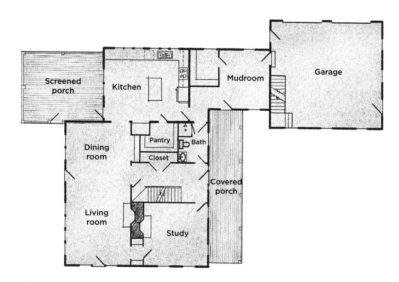

FIRST FLOOR

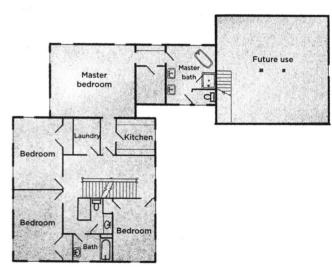

SECOND FLOOR

You can't see it from the front, but the house was positioned just so to take advantage of the sun: The metal roof on the back side contains two types of solar panels. From a design standpoint, the house is similar to many in the rural Northeast, where house and barn eventually become one space thanks to generations of additions. The house looks so authentic, people sometimes ask Sarah if she renovated an old house.

The only grass that gets mowed at the Crowells' new house is a skimpy swatch of ground immediately surrounding it. The rest of their land they let grow into a wild meadow, a natural habitat for the native birds and small wildlife that were there before the Crowells or anybody else arrived.

The Crowells save time, gas, and give back a little something.

It was this kind of thinking that got Sarah and Thomas Crowell into their new house. Both worked for environmental companies; both believed that when it came time to build a house, the house would be green. They wanted a home that would be an expression of their beliefs, while also providing a healthy environment and a good example for their two small children.

They decided to build the house in a way that created the least possible waste and used the least possible energy. They chose to position their new house on the land so that it took best advantage of the sun, and to install photovoltaic and solar hot water panels to generate as much of their own energy needs as possible (See Solar Demystified! sidebar, opposite). They focused on obtaining the most sustainable materials with which to build their home.

Choosing Panels

When they decided to build their new house, the Crowells lived in a Victorian house. It was drafty, the windows rattled, and the old steam boiler rumbled all night. At first they thought of remodeling it in a green way, but remodeling a structurally ornate Victorian house would be very difficult and hugely expensive. If they *built* a house, it could be as green and efficient as they wanted; it could have the traditional architecture they appreciated; it could be wherever they wanted it to be.

After reviewing options, the Crowells decided to build with panelized construction. They could get the traditional style they wanted, and a tight, energy-efficient house in a process that produces surprisingly little waste.

Connor Homes, the builder the Crowells selected, did most of the construction in a shop. The construction process was impressive. By building inside a protected environment, the panels and parts of their home were kept free from exposure to moisture and temperature extremes. Material use was efficient and waste was minimal. The design process was equally simple. Tom and Sarah sat down with the company's designer and, several e-mails later, the design was ready to be built.

In advance of the panels' arrival, insulated concrete forms for the foundation were set and filled with concrete. After the panels arrived from Vermont on two trucks, it took only five days to assemble the weathertight house. There were no dumpsters on-site because there was so little waste. With the little bit of leftover lumber, Thomas and his son built a tree house and a fenced run for their chickens.

BELOW The panels are stored upright in preparation for setting them on the foundation. (Photograph courtesy of Connor Homes)

BOTTOM Insulated concrete forms for the foundation were set and filled with concrete. (Photograph courtesy of Connor Homes)

A Traditional Natural Floor

Patented in England in 1863, Armstrong introduced linoleum to America in 1910. Although it fell out of favor in the United States decades ago, it has seen renewed interest because of its all-natural ingredients: linseed oil, powdered wood or cork, ground limestone, tree resin, and mineral pigments attached to jute fiber backing. Linoleum is recyclable, durable, resists burn marks, and its colors go all through the material. Linoleum also has anti-static properties so it doesn't attract and accumulate dust as easily as other flooring. It's available in tiles, or sheets in a variety of thicknesses, colors, and patterns.

Net Metering

Net metering programs let homeowners get credit for electricity they produce. Whether generated by solar, wind, or some other system, net metering can greatly offset the cost of a family's electricity, often with the meter spinning backwards when the system generates more electricity than the home uses. For information about the net metering policies and other financial incentives offered in various states, see www.dsireusa.org. For more on net metering, see www.eere.energy.gov or www.irecusa.org. In Canada, go to www.renewables.ca.

Solar Demystified!

When people talk about solar energy, they're often talking about a solar photovoltaic system (which creates electricity), or a solar thermal system (which heats water or air). Photovoltaic systems (PV) are composed of modules that convert sunlight to electricity, which can power all or a portion of a home's electrical system. Solar thermal systems (also called "solar hot water systems") are usually less expensive and more efficient than PV systems. Unlike PV panels, which are 14 to 16 percent efficient, solar thermal panels are about 92 percent efficient. These systems basically absorb the sun's rays to heat water, which can be used to heat the house or simply used as hot water. The Crowells have both systems on their roof. For information on rebates and incentives, see www.desireusa.org.

ABOVE The photovoltaic panels that generate electricity, to the left, share the rear roof with the passive solar hot water collectors. Lots of window area allows the owners to let in natural, warming sunlight.

OPPOSITE ABOVE LEFT The double-hung energy-efficient windows are traditional 12/12 divided lites, which bring a huge amount of light and warmth into the house. Great grandparents passed down the chandelier and side table. They found the dining table on Craigslist.

OPPOSITE ABOVE RIGHT From the refrigerator to the dishwasher, all appliances are ENERGY STAR rated for maximum energy efficiency. The light fixtures were reclaimed from an old school house. The wood flooring is reclaimed, antique pine.

OPPOSITE BELOW Most of the furnishings are either hand-me-downs from family members, reclaimed pieces, or goods from thrift, junk, and bargain stores.

Real Energy Efficiency

On a friend's advice, the couple insulated their house using a revolutionary spray-on foam, carrying the brand name of Icynene, a remarkable material that not only insulates a house to R-values usually exeeding fiberglass but, unlike fiberglass, it expands to completely fill and seal walls, preventing any heat-stealing air leaks.

The wall panels are made of 2x6 lumber, which lend themselves well to the Icynene. The walls are nice and thick with insulation near R-20. The Crowells did have to think through the electrical and plumbing layout (as well as anticipate future requirements), because walls packed with insulating foam make it difficult to make changes later. Just in case, Tom photographed the outer walls before they were insulated to create a visual map of all electrical and plumbing.

Quality construction, gap-free insulation, and a tightly sealed exterior envelope (as the outer "shell" of a house is sometimes called) are critical to energy efficiency. But if the rest of a home's details fail to follow suit, the outcome will disappoint. Energy-efficient windows and doors, a well-insulated foundation (see Insulated Concrete Form Foundations sidebar, page 25), and carefully chosen and installed heating, ventilating, and air conditioning systems are all equally important. The Crowells made sure that every component fit their energy-efficiency standards.

For the best air quality inside the house, they would need a continuous source of fresh air. One way to do so is to open windows and doors, though winters in upstate New York wouldn't allow that. Instead, the Crowells installed an energy recovery ventilator (ERV) (See Heat and Energy Recovery Ventilation Systems sidebar, page 85). The ventilator continuously exchanges stale indoor air with fresh outside air, all the while retaining any heated or cooled air.

BELOW Off the back of the house is the screened porch, where the family spends much of their time year-round. In mild weather, the openings hold screens; in cold seasons, the Crowells replace the screens with glass panels.

OPPOSITE Flooring in the front hall is reclaimed mushroom wood. The stairs were prebuilt in the Connor Shop and delivered to the site with doors and trim. The light fixture in the hallway is reclaimed.

Living off the Land

The Crowells wanted to be as self-sufficient as possible, which included reducing the amount of energy they needed. To take full advantage of sunlight, they planned for both passive and active solar energy. The active solar rooftop photovoltaic panels provide about half of their normal energy use. When the family leaves for vacation, their photovoltaics feed power back to their electric utility, reducing their electric bill (see Net Metering sidebar, page 107).

Solar hot water panels provide hot water for the family's daily needs, while also heating water for the radiant floor system and for the heat recovery system during the colder months. The state of New York subsidized about half of the cost of the photovoltaic panels. The Crowells received state and federal tax credits for both systems. They received the premium tax credit rate available because the house actually exceeded ENERGY STAR standards.

To take their self-sufficiency a bit further, the family keeps chickens and ducks to provide them with eggs. The Crowells are members of a Community Supported Agriculture (CSA) farm, which fulfills the family's produce needs—everything from apples to zucchini. Throughout the year they contribute their time to the farm.

Attention to Details

Sarah had a wonderful time decorating the house with used, reclaimed, and restored furnishings and fixtures. Craigslist.com, Habitat for Humanity's ReStores, flea markets, and thrift stores supplied things like the accent tiles they used for the bathrooms as well as old, one-of-a-kind light fixtures. Much of their furnishings came from relatives, including a dining room side table that had gone cross-country on a covered wagon.

The Crowells used the most natural and sustainable products they could find. For the play room, they chose cork flooring, which is a natural product, emits no VOCs, and is comfortable for sitting or standing. For the bathrooms, they chose natural linoleum flooring (see A Traditional Natural Floor sidebar, page 107) because it's made from linseed oil, requires little maintenance, and comes in a wide selection of colors.

And outside, the couple had to do very little landscaping to enjoy the natural beauty of their environment. The majority of the plants on their property are native to the area, and therefore require little care. That narrow swatch that they mow around their house is mainly to control ticks and yet give the kids a place to play outdoors.

The Method Cabin

Modular

PHOTOGRAPHER:

Lannie Boesiger

ARCHITECT:

Balance Associates

MANUFACTURER AND BUILDER:

Method Homes

LOCATION:

Glacier, Washington

SIZE:

1,811 square feet

GREEN ASPECTS:

FSC-certified wood

Passive solar

Cellulose insulation

Polyurethane insulation

Reclaimed cedar

ENERGY STAR-rated appliances

Energy-efficient lighting

Hydronic radiant heating

Eco-friendly counter tops

No-VOC paint

Low-VOC stains

CFL and halogen lighting

Standing seam metal roof

High-efficiency windows

Dual-flush toilets

Low-flow fixtures

High-efficiency boiler

Bamboo floors and cabinets

FLOOR PLAN

BELOW Because the house is in a flood plain, it's built up on a tall foundation, which gave Method a design opportunity.

OVERLEAF A window-filled bridge connects the master bedroom and common areas of the house to the two children's bedrooms.

Mark Rylant remembers an entire day spent carrying sheet after sheet of heavy, bulky drywall up three flights of stairs. There had to be a better job than construction laborer, he thought at the time. And there had to be a better way to build.

Over the years since, Mark has looked for new and innovative ways to add efficiency to construction (ways that didn't include hauling drywall up stairs). And after years of working on site-built construction—first for other companies, and then as an independent contractor—he found his *better way*.

Inspired by the growing number of modern prefab companies that have popped up all over the country, a light bulb (compact fluorescent, most likely) went off in Mark's head. Although, like many people, he had harbored a number of misconceptions about modular construction, these were shattered when he saw the quality and design coming out of these new companies.

Mark had grown tired of building in the rain and the mud. He decided to build modular homes. Teaming up with high school friend Brian Abramson, who had been working in commercial real estate and development, the partners found they had a passion for building prefab and for energy-efficient, healthy, durable construction, made with sustainable materials and minimum waste. The rest just came naturally.

A New Type of Factory

Unlike many established home construction factories, the one Mark and Brian created operates a bit differently. The partners leased a large facility, similar to most prefab factories, but decided to build their houses not with expensive, high-tech machines, but by hand, the way Mark built them on-site for years. They prefer hand building their houses, using the skills of master craftsmen, much the way houses are built in high-end timber frame shops.

Even without the sophisticated mechanization, they build a house in their factory in a quarter of the time it takes to build on-site. And their building materials are always indoors, out of the weather, so they don't soak up moisture that often leads to warping and twisting (a recipe for poor construction). On ordinary construction sites, wood can get wet, which often leads to mold and mildew problems in the finished house.

The Method Cabin was completed in three months with a 70 percent reduction in construction waste over a similar sized house. They achieved this simply by keeping tight control over details and quantities. Unlike modular companies that turn their houses over to a builder to complete, Method Homes maintains its own construction division to complete local projects. This way they maintain high quality and keep to schedule and budget.

Mark and Brian believe they have the ability to make an impact on the home building industry by making less of an impact on the *built* environment. Their motivation, they say, is their children, the next generation to inhabit the earth. They are concerned about the depletion of natural resources and our dependence on foreign oil.

OPPOSITE Simple, clean lines connect the dining area with the elevated deck, which is home to many a family cookout.

Standing-Seam Roofing

Metal is one of the most recyclable and durable materials in the world. And it's excellent for low-maintenance, long-lasting, fire-resistant, cost-effective roofing. It can be installed over existing roofing, reducing the amount of debris going into landfills. If effectively coated with zinc, aluminum, or aluminum alloy, metal roofs resist corrosion and last nearly indefinitely. A leading aluminum alloy roofing is Galvalume, which has 55 percent aluminum and 45 percent zinc alloy bonded to its steel base. A highly reflective paint, which is factory-applied to the surface, reflects sunlight and reduces heat transmission into the house. That, in turn, reduces the need for air conditioning. And though it may seem odd, steel roofs weigh only half as much as asphalt roofs, though they provide greater protection against snow, wind, ice, fire, and hail. Standing-seam panels run vertically, from the roof ridge to the eaves, and are interlocked with raised, overlapping seams and secured with long metal screws sealed by heavy rubber washers. Panels can be precut or cut on-site. To learn more, visit www.metalroofing.com.

Eco-friendly Countertops

The countertop materials that are currently available rival natural stone and other commonly used materials for good looks, price, and durability. These healthy and durable options are friendlier to the environment and fabricated using typical woodworking tools. One of the newest products, and the product used on the Method Cabin countertops, is called EcoTop. EcoTop is a fifty-fifty blend of Forest Stewardship Council–certified (FSC) bamboo fiber and recycled wood fiber salvaged from demolition sites. Binding them together are water-based resins, which are petroleum and VOC-free. Another material that has been available for several years is Paperstone, which is made from post-consumer waste, recycled paper, and petroleum-free phenolic resins. Both products earn points toward green certification. To learn more about these products, visit www.kliptech.com (for EcoTop) and www.paperstone.com.

A long, elevated countertop made of locally harvested maple divides the kitchen from the great room. The cabinets and flooring are bamboo. The other countertops are made from eco-friendly EcoTop.

To do their part, they intend to constantly look for new technologies and systems for creating better, healthier, and more responsibly built houses.

A Lighter Footprint

To build more responsibly, they choose materials and systems that conserve resources. They substantially cut down on waste by building in a controlled environment and carefully ordering materials to the required sizes (and there are never weather delays on their construction site). The standing-seam metal roof (see sidebar) is both durable and recyclable. All wood in the house is FSC-certified so they are assured it came from responsibly managed forests. The cedar siding was recycled from another construction project. Kitchen countertops are made from FSC-certified bamboo and recycled wood (see Eco-Friendly Countertops sidebar, opposite).

To save energy, they designed the envelope of the house as a well-insulated barrier against the elements. A combination of polyurethane foam and blown-in cellulose (see Old News is Good News sidebar, page 217) gives their walls an R-25 rating. With high-efficiency windows, and ENERGY STAR appliances and lighting, they save even more energy. The hydronic radiant system effectively heats the house using much less energy than traditional systems.

Brian and Mark's goal was to build the house as *green* as they possibly could. Currently, the partners are going through the process of having the house LEED certified.

Brian says building in a healthy, environmentally responsible way "should be prerequisites for any building in this day and age."

Farmhouse Bungalow

Structural Insulated Panels (SIPs)

MANUFACTURER:

Premier Panels

DESIGNER:

Peter Bergford

BUILDER:

Scott Homes, Inc.

LOCATION:

Olympia, Washington

SQUARE FOOTAGE:

1,728 square feet

CERTIFICATIONS:

Built Green–5 star

ENERGY STAR

GREEN ASPECTS:

Small footprint

Tankless water heater

Hydronic radiant floor

ENERGY STAR appliances & lighting

Reclaimed wood floors and antique pickle wood

Low-VOC paints

No-VOC finishes

High-efficiency fan

Low-flow toilets

FSC-certified wood

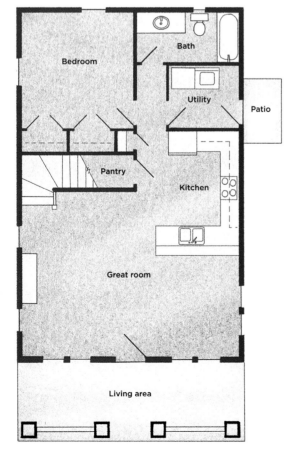

FIRST FLOOR

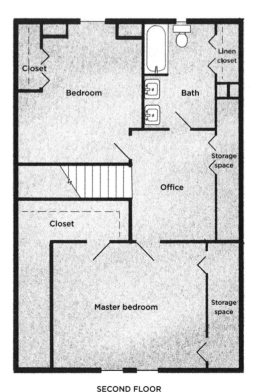

SECOND FLOOR

The house design replicates an old prairie farmhouse. The concrete walkway to the porch includes a carefully set stone surface. Traditional corbels, or brackets, both decorate and function structurally to support the porch overhang. (Photo by Dena Curtis)

Peter Bergford grew up in a Craftsman-style bungalow. He understood the charm of such a home and knew just how much living area could fit in its compact design.

So when his father, Scott Bergford, bought several buildable lots, Peter, the designer for Scott Homes, had an idea. His family's construction company would create a "bungalow village." They would build four bungalows, all from different eras, which together would create a tiny bungalow neighborhood.

His first design was this house, which Peter calls the Farmhouse Bungalow, reminiscent of his childhood home. Peter made diligent efforts to ensure the house had the proper proportions, height, and look of an authentic bungalow farmhouse. The lot is just 54 feet wide but looks bigger because Peter designed the house to measure only 24 feet across. This makes the Farmhouse narrower than most modern homes, but it remains true to the bungalow tradition of modest dimensions.

A SIPs Conversion

Scott had always built energy-efficient houses, though he'd built them on-site, the traditional way. But in the mid-1990s, a customer asked him to build a house of structural insulated panels (SIPs). Scott researched the technology and agreed, though he added a $5,000 premium to the cost. The extra money was to compensate for the "fear factor" of building with an unknown

product. The customer decided to go with traditional construction.

However, Scott's partner at the time was so impressed with what he'd learned about SIPs that he used them to build his own family home. The technology fulfilled all its stated advantages, proving energy efficient, quiet, cost effective, and fast to construct.

From then on, Scott built all his homes with SIPs. True to form, the Farmhouse Bungalow went up in five days. And it took only ten weeks from the groundbreaking until the final inspection.

An Authentic Design

Peter carefully maintained a farmhouse appearance for this first bungalow of the "village." For instance, in some cases he even modified some windows after installation so that they reflected the traditional bungalow look. Like many conventional bungalows—including the one where Peter grew up—two small windows flanked the fireplace, high on the wall. These provide indirect light as well as privacy.

He used wainscoting in the bathrooms, as was typical in old farmhouses. Authentic subway tile created a backsplash in the kitchen, and a modified antique maple buffet became the vanity in the downstairs bathroom, adding to the vintage charm of the house.

Beadboard and beams on ceilings also contribute to the authentic look. Wood reclaimed from old pickle vats was crafted into the fireplace

The main level of the house uses reclaimed FSC-certified fir flooring. Several coats of organic wax seal the floor, protect it, and give it a rich, natural luster. (Photo by Dena Curtis)

Hydronic versus Electric Radiant Heating

Radiant heat provides clean, even heat that warms objects in the room rather than the air, as forced hot air systems do. With radiant heat no pollutants are forced into the environment; the system also operates silently. Radiant systems can be easily zoned so that you only heat the areas you want. Radiant heat can be embedded in flooring, ceiling, or wall panels and can even be used to melt snow on driveways and sidewalks. Hydronic or hot water radiant systems can also heat pools, spas, and domestic hot water.

Radiant heat is either electric or hydronic. Though both work the same way, installations and operating costs differ vastly. Installing a gas-fired hydronic system is much more expensive, but costs less to operate. Electric systems install more easily and for less money, but are more expensive to operate, making them impractical for heating an entire house but effective for small areas, such as bathrooms. Both systems can be installed under most types of flooring, though electrical radiant heating is more appropriate for a remodel or retrofit. Hydronic systems are more complicated to install because they require a pump and special tubing to circulate water heated by an electric, gas, or oil-fired boiler. Hydronic systems adapt easily to hydronic solar panels and high-efficiency boilers, because they do not require high temperatures to operate. To learn more, visit www.radiantpanelassociation.org.

ABOVE A window seat showcased by wooden Craftsman-style columns adds charm to this upstairs children's room. All details were carefully designed for consistency with the original farmhouse bungalow design. (Photo by Mike Ryan)

OPPOSITE ABOVE Reflecting many of the qualities of traditional farmhouse bungalows, such as a farm sink, chicken-wire glass in the cabinets, retro light pendants, and wainscoting on the island, the kitchen is also filled with modern technology: ENERGY STAR appliances and a flat-screen television. (Photo by Dena Curtis)

OPPOSITE BELOW In keeping with the farmhouse style, two high windows flank the Rumford fireplace. The beaded and beamed ceiling also reflects traditional farmhouse design. The corbels beneath the mantel are both ornamental and structural, holding up the "pickle-wood" mantel shelf. (Photo by Mike Ryan)

The Blower Door Test

An energy-efficient house uses energy sparingly, but it must also conserve energy. Leaks in the exterior envelope of a house increase energy needs. To determine the extent of a home's air leaks, professionals conduct a blower door test, in which a powerful fan is mounted into an exterior door opening and sealed tightly to the frame. As the fan pulls air from the house, gauges measure the difference between indoor and outdoor air pressure to calculate the air leakage rate and to identify the leaks. Leaks are sealed and the test repeated. A common measure of this leakage is called "air changes per hour," or ACH, and represents the number of times the air inside a house is exchanged with outside air. While an old house might have as many as 8 ACH, the Farmhouse Bungalow scored a 1.7 ACH. More air changes mean leakier homes, higher fuel costs, and greater potential for moisture intrusion. To find certified contractors to perform a blower door test on your home, visit www.resnet.us.

Count Rumford's Fireplace

In the eighteenth century, Benjamin Thompson, an American who had sided with the British during the Revolution and fled to Europe, took the name Count Rumford. Although mostly self-taught, Rumford garnered renown for his work on the nature of heat. He designed a fireplace with a shallow floor, angled walls, and a restricted opening into the flue, all of which radiated more heat into the house than up the chimney. The fireplace was more efficient but also did a better job of venting smoke. His design made him famous throughout Europe and North America, where Thomas Jefferson used Rumford's principles to build all the fireplaces at Monticello. Rumford fireplaces are among the few fireplaces to be tested for emissions and certified in Washington state. For further information, visit www.rumford.com.

mantel and into treads on the stairs, adding both a touch of antiquity and one more note of greenness. Peter searched the Internet to find genuine chicken-wire glass, which he installed in some of the kitchen cabinet doors. A farmhouse sink cemented the look of a real farmhouse kitchen.

In a nod to modern technology, a flat video screen was hardwired into the kitchen wall, where it serves both as a television and as a computer monitor. Along with the feel of the old, this little bungalow has all the modern conveniences homeowners have come to expect and enjoy.

Keeping It Comfortable

Unlike typical drafty farmhouses, the Farmhouse Bungalow boasts great energy efficiency, due to efforts by Scott and Peter. Like they do for all their homes, the Bergfords took a whole-house approach to creating a healthy, energy-efficient environment.

A hydronic radiant system heats the house (see Hydronic versus Electric Radiant Heating sidebar, page 125), supplied by a tankless, gas-fired water heater that also produces enough hot water for domestic use. A highly efficient Rumford fireplace (see Count Rumford's Fireplace sidebar, page 126) adds to the aesthetics and supports the efficiency of the home.

The Bergfords used double-pane, low-E, argon gas-filled windows throughout. The vinyl windows are economical, low maintenance, ENERGY STAR rated, and compatible with the traditional look of the house. Thanks to the use of tightly-fitted SIPs, no air infiltration steals the home's conditioned air.

A blower door test scored the house a 1.7 air changes per hour (or ACH; see The Blower Door Test sidebar, opposite). To qualify for an ENERGY STAR rating, a house must score 7 ACH or less. The Farmhouse Bungalow proved at least 50 percent more efficient than the model house offered as a standard of energy efficiency for Washington state. Because of the bungalow's high efficiency, Scott Homes qualified for a $2,000 federal tax credit, which Scott says he receives on every home he builds. According to the home's owners, heating costs run about $200 a year, far less than that required to keep a typical house this size comfortable in the colder months. The house was built ready for solar panels, which if installed would decrease the energy costs further.

Besides qualifying for an ENERGY STAR rating, the Farmhouse Bungalow received the highest Built Green rating of 5 stars, a program now recognized in a number of states. It also won multiple awards from the Olympia Master Builders, a division of the National Association of Home Builders, for "Best of Show," "Best Curb Appeal," and "Best Kitchen."

The Wave Cottage

Modular

PHOTOGRAPHER:

Jack Gardner Photography
(unless otherwise noted)

DESIGNER:

pv+r

MANUFACTURER:

Nationwide Homes

BUILDER:

Wave Construction

LOCATION:

WaterSound, Florida

SIZE:

1,365 square feet

RATINGS:

Fortified. . .for safer living

GREEN ASPECTS:

A/C in conditioned space

Bio-based foam insulation

Conditioned attic

Energy Recovery Ventilator (ERV)

No-VOC paint

No particle board/formaldehyde

No carpet

Aluminum clad impact doors and windows

CFL lighting

Screened porches

Cross ventilation

Low-flow faucets

High-efficiency HVAC

Detached garage

ENERGY STAR ceiling fans

ENERGY STAR appliances and lighting

Walkable community with park in front

Small footprint

Efficiency of space

Siding from reclaimed or downed lumber

FLOOR PLAN

OPPOSITE ABOVE The garage was site-built, but designed to exceed local building codes and to withstand winds of 160 miles per hour. The garage is separated from the house to prevent toxic fumes from entering the living space.

OPPOSITE BELOW House and landscape require little maintenance. The aluminum-clad windows and doors necessitate as little maintenance as the natural habitat surrounding the house.

Scott Henson and his partners in Wave Construction set a goal to build the greenest affordable house in the Florida seaside community of WaterSound.

The partners knew they could build an expensive house (most of the houses Scott has built in the area cost up to $400 per square foot), but they wanted this house to cost no more than $190 per square foot. So they needed high-quality construction at a reasonable price. The biggest obstacle was the limited availability of skilled carpenters in the area; it would be expensive to bring in the craftsmen they needed.

The elegant solution? High-quality, energy-efficient, green, and affordable modular construction. And Henson insists that quality saw no sacrifice in the process.

Sturdy Building Blocks

Nationwide Homes constructed the modulars, or "boxes," which came stripped—no windows, doors, siding, or finishes. Wave Construction worried that factory quality wouldn't meet their standards, so they chose to do much of the finish themselves. After working with the modular factory, however, they say they now have confidence in the quality of modular construction and in the future will have the modular manufacturer more completely build the house before shipping.

Scott and his partners wanted the house to be beautiful—which it is—but it had to be energy efficient and stand up against the harshest weather conditions of coastal Florida. They decided to have the house Fortified . . . for safer living by the Institute for Business and Home Safety (see Protection from the Elements sidebar, opposite). Scott wanted this house to exceed local building code requirements because he hoped to dispel "naysayers' preconceived notions about modular construction."

The house would cost about 10 to 20 percent more to qualify as fortified, but with the significant premium break Scott received from the insurance company for the certification, he believes the payback will come in as little as three years.

And construction happened quickly. The three boxes that constitute the house were set in about four hours and all the rest of the work completed in under a month—very fast by any standard.

Designing Small

Wave built the house in an upscale community, as a prototype. Because the land alone cost so much, Scott planned to maximize the home's useful space inside. He minimized the hallways. The living spaces—living room, dining room, and kitchen—were all incorporated into one big room.

WaterSound community guidelines require porches, but the designers and owners opted for larger porches than mandated on the front and rear of the house to extend the living space. The master bedroom and bath were designed like a hotel suite, with a large opening between them to open up the space and make the rooms feel

To make the least possible impact on the property, the house was lowered carefully onto the prepared foundation. Unlike most modular houses built today, this house was delivered without windows, doors, and much of the detail work. (Photograph courtesy of Vicky Patterson)

Curly Bulbs

Promoting compact fluorescent bulbs (CFLs) in this book is probably preaching to the choir—more than likely you already have CFLs in most of your sockets—but a few things about these bulbs are worth repeating. CFLs are now available for virtually every home fixture, from tiny, decorative lighting to big flood lights. These little miracles use 75 percent less juice than incandescent bulbs, last 10 times longer, and produce 75 percent less heat (important when you're running an air conditioner). And think about this: If every house swapped out just one old-style bulb with a CFL, America would use $600 million less electricity and halt enough harmful emissions to equal removing eight hundred thousand cars from the road.

Protection from the Elements

To protect their house from the hurricanes and strong wind that afflict the Gulf Coast, the owners strove to exceed the Florida Building Code. They chose to have the house Fortified . . . for safer living, a program established by the Institute for Business and Home Safety (IHBS), a nonprofit dedicated to better building practices. The house was engineered to withstand winds up to 160 miles per hour. As required by the program, a secondary water barrier sits under the roofing, a peel and stick continuous membrane, rather than standard overlapping sheets of tarpaper. That rests atop 3/4-inch plywood, stronger and heavier than the standard 1/2-inch oriented strand board. The windows and doors are impact resistant. Insulation in the attic and crawl space is dense and effective spray foam. The steel strapping holding the house to the foundation doubles the requirement of the local code. To learn more about Fortified, visit www.disastersafety.org.

RIGHT The screened front porch becomes a less formal extension of the house and a place where the family can cool off, relax, and enjoy the nature free of bugs.

OPPOSITE ABOVE By combining the living room, dining room, and kitchen into one open space, Scott and his partners made the house feel larger than it is.

OPPOSITE BELOW LEFT Two smaller doors between the master bedroom and bathroom create a larger opening between the two rooms when needed and gobble up less space when open.

OPPOSITE BELOW RIGHT Designed with a small footprint to avoid useless unused space, the house also includes many windows to provide excellent cross ventilation and plenty of natural light. The kitchen, dining, and living room area inhabit one big, light-filled space.

bigger. Instead of one large door, which would eat up floor space with its wide swing; two small doors solved the problem.

Vacation Home at Last

Traci and Tyler Holstein fell in love with what they call their "sweet little house."

They had wanted a vacation house close to Rosemary Beach, an area that appealed to them because of the quiet it would provide when they made the trip from their primary residence in Amarillo, Texas.

The excellent construction also drew the Holsteins to the compact house. Traci appreci-

ated that her house, unlike a house built on-site through all kinds of weather, never suffered from exposure to the elements. And both husband and wife are happy it was built so strong. It provides Traci peace of mind that the house will weather whatever comes even when she, her husband, and their two small children are back home in Texas.

They've been through a few good storms in the house, Traci says, and even when the wind is howling, the house remains peacefully quiet. The couple also appreciates the low electric bill, ranging from $35 to $75 a month, far less than they pay in Texas.

EcoFabulous House

Modular

PHOTOGRAPHERS:

Martin Tessler, Bob Matheson,

(unless otherwise noted)

ARCHITECT:

Kanau (Kon) Uyeyama

MANUFACTURER:

Shelter Industries, Inc.

BUILDER:

Architecton/Shelter Industries

LOCATION:

Vancouver, British Columbia

SIZE:

1,400 square feet

RATINGS:

Gold Star (BC Hydro)

BuiltGreenBC–eligible

GREEN ASPECTS:

Small eco-footprint

Sustainable and recycled materials

Sprinkler system

Energy-efficient lighting, appliances, windows, and fireplace

Integrated home control system

Minimal or zero VOCs

Low-VOC paint

Cabinets made of 100 percent recycled paper

Local products

Water conservation

Continuous ventilation

Hydronic heating system

Individual thermostats for radiators

Solar panels for hot water

Galvanized steel roof

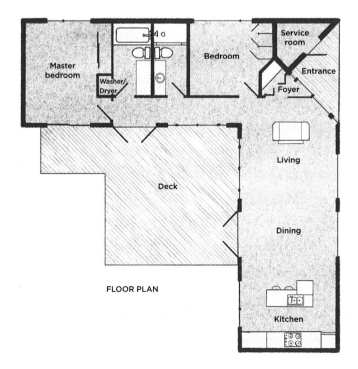

FLOOR PLAN

BELOW An aerial view of the house shows how the two modules work together to form a courtyard, with walls of windows opening onto it. (Photo by Bob Matheson)

OVERLEAF A dropped, curvy ceiling adds visual interest to the long and narrow bedroom wing hall. (Photo by Bob Matheson)

Some of the furniture was made from recycled material and is itself recyclable. The fireplace uses electronic ignition instead of a pilot light to save on gas. (Photo by Bob Matheson)

In 2002, Mary Todd, textbook author and medical school professor at the University of British Columbia, retired. But her plans did not include catching up on her reading or starting a new hobby. Instead, Mary joined her architect husband, Kon Uyeyama, on a second career: designing and promoting energy- and resource-efficient houses.

They had always been ecologically minded, before those words were even defined. They'd grown organic vegetables since they designed and built their first house in 1976. They turned off lights when not in use, had different thermostats for different areas of the house, and composted everything possible.

As two people with a single purpose, they could accomplish more toward their new calling working as a committed pair than they could individually.

Show Business

One day in 2008, Mary heard that the Greater Vancouver Home Builders' Association, a sponsor of the BC Home and Garden Show, wanted an eco-friendly, modular, avant-garde house to display at the show. The house had to look different from an ordinary home-show house. Mary called to let them know she had just what they wanted.

In the past, Mary and Kon had worked with Shelter Industries, a local modular company, and they approached the company's president, Harold Clifford, to combine efforts. They chose modular because of its intrinsically green character: mate-

rials constructed indoors and protected from the elements; waste kept to a minimum. The couple had used eco-friendly products and materials in projects, but this house had to surpass anything they had achieved before. They would "take this house to the next level" ecologically, Mary said.

A Design Is Born

First, Mary and Kon wanted the house to be simple. The couple started with two rectangles that joined at the main entry to form a V-shape. In the crook of this 90-degree angle would be a 400-square-foot courtyard deck that would offer multiple access ways to the house and create an indoor/outdoor living environment.

Kon wanted the house to be as energy efficient as possible. As he designed it, the shed roofs bend in at the ends to enclose the energy inside. A highly efficient hydronic heating system provides radiant and convection heat from thin radiators that are each equipped with its own thermostat (the bathroom radiators also provide the luxury of heated towels). Rooftop solar panels heat the water, but they can be supplemented by the gas-fired hydronic system. The system also heats water for the deck spa.

Other details include a gas fireplace with an electronic ignition in place of a pilot light; typical pilot lights use as much gas when the fireplace is not in use as the fireplace itself uses in a year. Compact fluorescent lighting and LED lighting was used throughout, further reducing energy use. Lights are controlled by an integrated con-

Buying Locally

Buying locally avoids the pollution created by trucks delivering materials a long distance. Local materials are easy to return if problems arise and the support benefits local economies. Mary and Kon bought locally whenever possible. For instance, the concrete tiles on the fireplace and foyer were handmade locally using recycled material. The siding and decking are made from local British Western red cedar and all exterior lighting was produced in Vancouver. The countertops and tub surrounds were also made locally, and the kitchen and bathroom cabinets were fabricated in Vancouver.

The Speed of Modular

Construction of the EcoFabulous house began December 3, 2007, and the structure was delivered to the Home and Garden Show on February 11, 2008—nearly complete with only hook-ups and landscaping left to do. This is a wonderful example of a key feature of modular construction: speed of completion.

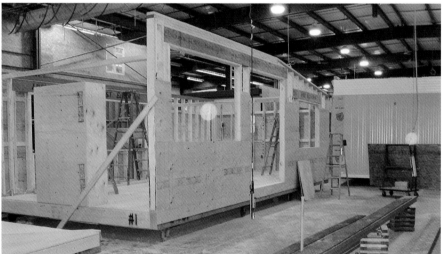

trol system, which has the capacity to expand for other uses to meet the needs of future residents.

The system can adapt to add cameras to monitor the house via the Web when the residents are away. It can also shut off power to the television and other entertainment components, which eat up a lot of energy even when not in use. And it can control the indoor environment by responding to the outdoor temperature. The system can manage security and computer equipment. Designed for personalization, this integrated control system can add to the casual and comfortable environment the house was built to create.

Mary and Kon selected everything in the house to be as efficient and environmentally kind as possible. Kitchen appliances, windows, and the fireplace are energy efficient. Windows are double-paned, low-E, and argon-filled for maximum efficiency. The dishwasher uses a minimal amount of water and both bathrooms include low-flush toilets.

Home as Art

From the bright green entrance to the vibrant purple inside, the house exudes a modern, creative, and joyful mood. Mary and Kon intended the house to be eco-friendly—that was a given. But Kon wanted it to be an artistic house as well. He embellished the hips, or joints of the roof, with fins to emphasize the metal roof. He turned the window wall into a sculptural element with lateral bracings and iridescent plastic insets.

ABOVE Interior designer Daine Halley selected not only cheerful colors for the furnishings but also as eco-friendly as possible. (Photo by Martin Tessler)

OPPOSITE TOP AND CENTER The structure of the modules was built in the Shelter Industries facility. (Photos by Architecton)

OPPOSITE BOTTOM The modules of the house are stacked on flatbed trucks for delivery to the convention center. (Photograph courtesy of Architecton)

The dropped, curvy ceiling in the bedroom wing hall brings visual delight to the long and narrow passageway. Bright colors on walls and doors add an element of surprise and serve as an economical way to add drama to the design without adding cost.

Inside, the couple wanted the furnishings to be comfortable and cheerful, but they also wanted them as green and sustainable as the house. Interior designer Daine Halley selected the most eco-friendly materials possible, and her choices cover a broad range. Daine included millwork from sustainably harvested engineered wood veneer, kitchen and bath tiles that are partially recycled, and fabrics created from recycled content that can themselves be recycled at the end of their life cycle.

Health, Safety, and Native Plants

Health and safety were important considerations in the design of the house. For safety, Kon and Mary incorporated a fire sprinkler system with heads that are flush with the ceiling, making them unobtrusive. Because the home was designed as a vacation retreat, a sprinkler system (see About Fire Sprinkler Systems sidebar, page 56) would give the homeowners peace of mind when the house was unoccupied.

To maintain good indoor air quality, workers used all zero- or minimal-VOC paints and continued with many other products used in the construction, such as the one hundred percent recycled paper cabinets in the kitchen and bath-

room. A passive, continuously operating ventilation system assures the homeowners of enough fresh air even when windows and doors are closed in winter. (see Central Exhaust Ventilation sidebar, opposite).

Houston Landscapes, and Arcon Rock and Waterscapes planted drought-resistant grasses and plants around the house. When the house reaches its final destination, the driveway will be made of porous pavers that allow rainwater to quickly go back into the ground to help recharge aquifers. All plantings are native to the area and therefore use a minimum of water.

The house can support a graywater system to decrease demands on the local water supply. To avoid light pollution of the night sky, low-wattage CFLs were used outside (see Dark Sky Lighting sidebar, opposite). All fixtures were designed to accept only CFLs, so there's no place an energy-hogging incandescent bulb can hide.

Roughly 63,000 people visited the Home and Garden Show. Visitors agreed that this was the best house ever presented at the show: adjectives ranged from "exciting" to "spectacular."

After the show, the EcoFabulous House was taken by flatbed truck back to Shelter Industries, where it will be stored until it finds a permanent home.

BELOW Dark sky–friendly exterior lights reduce nighttime light pollution. (Photograph courtesy of Architecton)

BOTTOM The kitchen cabinets are made from recycled paper covered with a photo-imprinted veneer of teak and emit zero VOCs. Tiles are made from recycled glass and the flooring is cork, made from the renewable bark of cork oak trees. (Photo by Martin Tessler)

Dark Sky Lighting

Light pollution from overly bright or misdirected outdoor lighting creates glare, shines unwanted light into neighboring houses, and wastes billions of dollars in electricity as it overpowers even the moon and stars. Excess light may pose a health risk because our bodies, which require a certain amount of darkness, aren't always getting it. Plants and animals exposed to night light may also be harmed. And light pollution prevents people from seeing the heavens above—the awesome and infinite natural phenomenon that has amazed and confounded humans for thousands of years.

New fixtures and design techniques can minimize wasted and unwanted light. These "dark sky–friendly" fixtures direct light down, not up or sideways. Reduced wattage also reduces night glare, which makes it more difficult to see. Photo controls and movement sensors on exterior lights provide safety and security while reducing energy use, because lights only shine when needed. Many communities have adopted ordinances that require dark-sky features. The International Dark-Sky Association provides an extensive list of manufacturers who get their Seal of Approval. To learn more, visit their Web site at www.darksky.org.

Central Exhaust Ventilation

An energy-efficient house with a tight exterior envelope needs fresh air. Central exhaust ventilation systems provide it. The system draws stale air from the bathrooms and kitchen using a central fan located in an attic, basement, crawl space, or mechanical room (where it's housed in this structure). The fan propels stale air outside while creating a slight negative pressure that sucks fresh air into the house through inlets located on the upper walls of all central living spaces. These systems improve air quality and the respiratory health of the inhabitants. They are normally run continually during the heating season, when doors and windows are more likely to be closed.

Glen Cairn Cottage

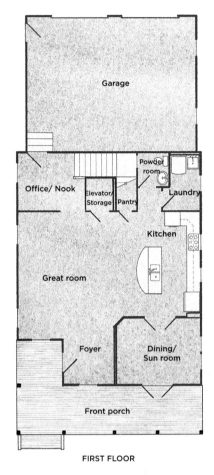

FIRST FLOOR

Garage

Office/ Nook

Elevator/ Storage

Pantry

Powder room

Laundry

Kitchen

Great room

Foyer

Dining/ Sun room

Front porch

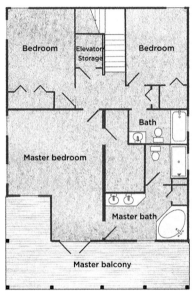

SECOND FLOOR

Bedroom

Elevator/ Storage

Bedroom

Bath

Master bedroom

Master bath

Master balcony

Modular

PHOTOGRAPHER:

Jim Goins Photography

DESIGNER:

Carl Krave

MANUFACTURER:

Nationwide Custom Homes

BUILDER:

Pocket Neighborhoods, Inc.

LOCATION:

Dunedin, Florida

SIZE:

1,988 square feet

RATINGS:

Green Home and Green Development Certification by the Florida Green Building Coalition

GREEN ASPECTS:

Salvaged existing structures on the property

GREENGUARD-certified by the GREENGUARD Environmental Institute (GEI) insulation*

High-efficiency HVAC

Tankless water heater

ENERGY STAR hurricane impact windows

Insulated exterior doors

Low-flow showerheads

Dual-flush toilets

Permeable crushed oyster shell walkway

Large porches

ENERGY STAR appliances

Universal design elements

*The GREENGUARD Environmental Institute is an independent, nonprofit organization that oversees the GREENGUARD Certification Program, which establishs acceptable standards for indoor products and testing protocols.

Developer Carl Krave wanted to build houses that would endure for generations.

It was a practical goal, but also, he felt, a morally responsible one. If successful, he would "prove to people that one can build a very efficient, very attractive, maintenance-free green house."

In an earlier career, Carl produced annual reports for big companies like Hershey Foods. It was lucrative but extremely wasteful. By the time they were printed, the annual reports were virtually out of date—and what wasn't mailed out got trashed. In his new pursuit, Carl would do things differently.

All Green

He bought land in Dunedin, Florida, north of Clearwater, a spot nicely set a couple of blocks between downtown and the intercoastal waterway. Excellent restaurants and shops bustle nearby in walking distance—an important element of Carl's plan.

He spent several years getting all the necessary town approvals for the community he planned. When it all was approved, he intended to build the first certified green development in the county.

The lot already held three salvageable houses. Carl moved two of them to a lot nearby. The third he kept on the property as his office. Simply by preserving the three structures, Krave prevented many tons of debris from ending up in

a landfill. In the process, he also preserved two 1921 cottages, little bits of local history.

As he sees it, preserving those two cottages not only kept them out of the landfill, but also retained the "embodied energy" they represent: the materials and labor it took to construct them. Carl renovated one of the houses, bringing it back to near original condition; the second cottage he sold to a contractor, who planned to renovate it.

Compact Convenience

Carl designed his little community densely, without a lot of wasted space, on 2 acres with 15 feet between each of the fourteen houses that will eventually share the central courtyard. The community is built for walking—to visit neighbors, to town, to the nearby waterfront.

Without using some of the more expensive energy-saving technology, such as geothermal systems, Carl made the houses extremely energy efficient. He created a tight envelope around each house, with a keen eye to the details that went into roof, windows and doors, walls, insulation, and foundation.

High-efficiency insulation filled every outside wall or surface. High-efficiency windows, combined with a radiant barrier inside the roof (which blocks up to 97 percent of the radiant energy from entering the attic in hot, humid Florida), were part of the plan. To save additional energy, Carl included a tankless water heater, which uses about 40 percent less energy than conventional water heaters, and a high-efficiency

PREVIOUS LEFT PAGE A 200-ton crane gently sets the first 64-foot module in place onto its foundation. The house was completely set in about 10 hours.

PREVIOUS PAGE Generous wrap-around porches on both floors bring the outside in. Low-E French doors make alfresco dining a reality in the first-floor dining room, while the same energy-saving doors in the master suite invite the homeowner to spend lazy Sunday mornings in a private, personal oasis with coffee and a newspaper.

OPPOSITE Airy 9-foot ceilings and a large "plantation" fan add a feeling of spaciousness as they supplement the central air conditioning system.

Dual-Flush Toilets

Dual-flush toilets make so much sense. After all, why should every flush use the same amount of water? These "two-speed" toilets are now readily available from many manufacturers, in a variety of styles, colors, and price ranges. They look like traditional toilets except for the flushing handle, or button, which lets you select the volume of water used for the flush. The short flush uses 0.8 gallons of water; the long flush uses 1.6 gallons of water, which saves up to 8,000 gallons of water annually. These toilets have been available in Europe for years and are even mandatory in Israel for new or replacement toilets.

Permeable Drives and Walks

In the Glen Cairn community, crushed oyster shells pave walks and drives. It's a plentiful material that rainwater flows right through, to be naturally filtered on its way into the ground. Asphalt and concrete don't allow water to seep into the ground, but rather force it into manmade channels, collecting surface pollutants along the way. A variety of so-called pervious paving materials are on the market—including porous grass pavers, gravel, and crushed stone. Though these generally cost as much as 40 percent more than asphalt surfaces, many are maintenance free. To learn more about permeable paving materials, visit www.toolbase.org.

With the dining room placed between the kitchen and the front deck, French doors on both sides allow the homeowner to treat the space as an "outdoor room" when weather permits. Low-E eyebrow windows bathe the room with light while maintaining privacy from the neighbor next door.

LEFT Eyebrow windows bathe the kitchen with early morning sunshine from the eastern side of the house. All appliances are ENERGY STAR rated. As Florida's first Gold Certified Water Star home, a water-saving dishwasher and low-flow faucet aerators were added to enhance water conservation.

BOTTOM The spacious second floor porch encourages cozy, private moments, undisturbed by any activity below.

HVAC system. Low-flow showerheads and dual-flush toilets minimize water consumption.

Shortly after the model house was set, some local builders, some with more than thirty years' experience, came to see what the fuss was about. They wanted to see what a modular house looked like and what Carl meant when he said they were "built green." He showed them exactly what he meant.

Carl set out to create an example that would act as a guidepost for others. He believes his little community makes good sense, works for its inhabitants, and will be around for generations.

Since his first house went up, his development has won two Aurora Awards, issued by the Southeast Building Conference. The Southwest Florida Water Management District also chose the house as its first Water Star Gold Certified home. Several other design and building awards are pending.

3

GREENEST HOUSES

As consumers become more knowledgeable about their options, they look for builders who can create the houses they want. As a result, homes get greener and greener, and the market for environmentally conscious construction expands.

For instance, Ferrier Custom Builders, which built Heather's Home, is increasingly in demand. Much of the company's business comes through word of mouth, without bids or a formal process. Consumers seek out builders who understand green design and construction and the importance of energy efficiency, resource conservation, and waste reduction.

Every year, more municipalities require that new construction adheres to an environmental standard, whether it's ENERGY STAR ratings, required for all new houses in several towns on Long Island, New York, or a regional program, such as the GreenPoint Rated system used in parts of California. As government steps in, states and counties are establishing programs to evaluate and document the green aspects of home construction.

Here's a remarkable statistic: More than five hundred regional and national rating systems for green construction now exist. A decade ago, those could be counted on one hand. An example of a house built to a regional rating system is the mkLotus, built to comply with California's GreenPoint Rated system.

In the United States, two national programs are growing in recognition. In 2007, the United States Green Building Council established guidelines (the Leadership in Energy and Environmental Design, or LEED, rating system) for the construction of green housing on a national level. LEED has four levels: certified, silver, gold, and platinum. Several of the houses in this book have met these requirements at various levels of LEED: the Living Home, Highland House, PowerHouse, EcoUrban House, Back from the Burn, Heather's Home, and The Mountain House

In 2008, the National Association of Home Builders added a certification program to verify green construction on four levels: bronze, silver, gold, and emerald. The program operates in a way similar to the LEED program, but works more closely with state and local NAHB groups to help builders and consumers meet their requirements. Because the program is new, few houses in this book have been certified other than The Mountain House. But several other houses in this chapter also meet their standards.

Like many of the programs, the NAHB guidelines—the National Green Building Standard—uses a point-based system. They offer points for prefabricated construction methods. A panelized roof or an advanced wall framing system gets 6 points; modular construction earns 13 points, the single highest-point award in the program. These systems award points to builders who reduce material use and construction waste. 8 points go to a SIPs-constructed house because of its substantially increased R-value and energy efficiency.

The Solar Decathlon, an educational project of the U.S. Department of Energy, offers university students the opportunity to learn firsthand the challenges of building self-sufficient houses that function off the grid. LEAFHouse, built by students at the University of Maryland, is one of the finest participants in the event and an example of the future potential of home building.

This section includes some of the greenest houses in North America, most of which have been certified by a state or national program. Like all the houses in this book, the houses in this section were constructed using impressive new products and building techniques, some of which seem so simple and natural that people may wonder why it took so long for word to get out.

If you're interested in finding a manufacturer to build a green, prefabricated home, you can locate them through the Building Systems Councils of the NAHB. To learn more about certification, you can check with your local chapter of the NAHB or speak with your builder. Or just look in the back of this book for the address or URL you need to get started.

Heather's Home

Structural Insulated Panels (SIPs)

PHOTOGRAPHER:

Terri Glanger Photography

(unless otherwise noted)

ARCHITECT:

Gary Gene Olp; GGOArchitects, Corp.

MANUFACTURER:

FisherSIPs

BUILDER:

Ferrier Custom Homes

LOCATION:

Lake Weatherford, Texas

SIZE:

2,028 square feet

RATINGS:

ENERGY STAR; LEED-H—Platinum

GREEN ASPECTS:

Passive solar design

Structural Insulated Panels

Energy Recovery Ventilator (ERV)

High-efficiency heating and cooling system

Dual-flush toilets

Low-flow faucets and showers

Rainwater catchment system

Solar hot water heater

ENERGY STAR windows and doors

ENERGY STAR appliances

ENERGY STAR lighting

No-or low-VOC paints and stains

Fiber cement siding

Proper shading of windows and doors

Whole-house fans

Concrete floors

Regional white ash cabinetry

Galvalume standing seam metal roof

Drought-tolerant native plants

Bamboo flooring

Recycled sheetrock and Hardiboard made into mulch for landscaping

PET carpet

Pervious walk and driveways

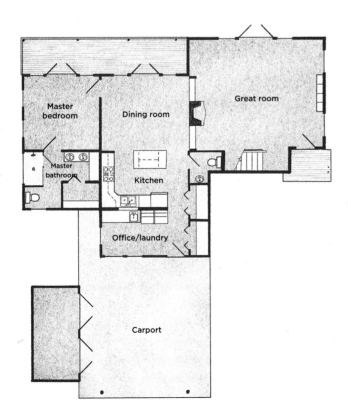

FIRST FLOOR

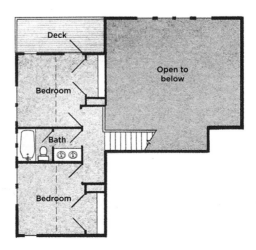

SECOND FLOOR

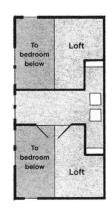

THIRD FLOOR

A design highlight of the house is the scattering of small windows in the two-story, north-facing living room wall. If these windows faced south or west, they would draw in too much sun and heat up the house in the Texas summer.

While working for her builder father, Heather Ferrier watched as one gorgeous house after another took shape under his careful oversight. But when it was time for Heather to have her own home, she didn't want just another beautiful house. She wanted more. And less.

The result was exactly what she wanted. The stunning window-studded modern design made of prefabricated panels fulfilled a dream and accomplished a mission: have more, use less. The more was style, sustainability, efficiency, and livability. The less was decreased waste in the landfill, less energy required, less water used, less maintenance necessary, and less time to build. In Heather's house, less became more.

Borrowing a page from father Don Ferrier's playbook, Heather made sure that the house she would build for herself and her sister was designed with a "whole-house mentality." She wanted green to run deep in the design; the materials, the finishes, and the systems—electrical, plumbing, insulation, heating, ventilation, and air conditioning. The whole house would be green; not just green on the surface, but through and through.

So when her father began building a house for architect Gary Olp that encompassed much of what Heather wanted for her own house, Heather asked Olp to design her house like his, but to match it to her small budget. The result was a contemporary home with an open floor plan, lots of windows, and a passive solar approach to temperature control.

Green Speed

Heather believed in her house and in her vision for it. To prove her commitment, she raced the clock to complete the house in time for the Greater Fort Worth Builders Association spring tour of homes. Construction began in January and ended a little more than three months later—a job that would've taken three or four times that for a conventional house.

Her choice of structural insulated panels (SIPs) allowed the rapid schedule. SIPs go up fast because they are precisely cut in a factory to blueprint specifications, trucked to the site, hoisted into place, and fastened securely. Panels provide superb insulation, great strength, reduced noise inside the house, and reduced job-site waste, which can fill multiple dumpsters in standard construction.

Like clockwork, Heather's panels were delivered to the site with all the openings pre-cut, hoisted by a crane, and assembled like big puzzle pieces atop the pre-poured foundation in only five days. By the time of the home tour, Heather's house was home-show ready.

Hers was the only green house on the tour, where more than five thousand people saw just how far green design had come. "My house was a launching pad for (local) public awareness," Heather said. "It was a project people could really identify with" because, while it was more contemporary than other houses on the tour, she believed people felt comfortably at home in her house.

OPPOSITE The small windows along the staircase light the space naturally. The flooring is easy-to-clean stained concrete. A ceiling fan moves air to make Heather and her guests cooler while using less energy than air conditioning.

Catching H2O

Before modern plumbing, people collected rainwater for drinking and household use. Given the cost and diminishing supply of fresh water, rainwater collection again makes sense. Collecting rainwater puts less pressure on municipal water systems, mitigates urban flooding, and provides water for irrigation and other household needs.

A rainwater system includes a catchment area (usually the roof), gutters to carry the water to a cistern or tank for storage, and a filter system. With minimum treatment, rainwater can be used for gardening, toilets, and laundry. A more complex, expensive, and maintenance-intensive sanitary treatment is required to make water safe for bathing and human consumption. With the variety of local codes regulating these systems, the local building or health department should be contacted before planning a rainwater harvesting system.

Daylighting

Daylighting is the practice of lighting an interior using natural light rather than electric light whenever possible. Natural light is usually more pleasing, reduces electric use, reduces heat created by artificial lighting, and connects indoors with outdoors. Studies show daylighted schools and offices have increased productivity. Heather's house was oriented to take the best advantage of the sun, and all the windows arranged to grab as much daylight as possible.

Affirmative Action

Heather didn't wake up one morning knowing how to plan a green house. But she knew enough to be aware she needed help. Working with Building America, a program sponsored by the United States Department of Energy, and with the building technology-consulting firm Building Science Corporation (BSC), Heather learned which housing components offered the best payback. In her case, that meant investments that paid for themselves in five years or less. (She avoided non-investment upgrades like fancy countertops and other pricey finishes.)

Building America and BSC worked alongside Heather and Olp, reviewing drawings and offering suggestions on window design, size, and placement, which Heather adjusted throughout the house based on their calculations.

Every choice Heather made for her house, each decision large or small, passed through a green filter. A choice was either rejected or selected based on its earth-friendliness and energy efficiency. Rooftop solar panels provide hot water. A rainwater catchment system (see sidebar, page 155) harvests the falling rain for watering lawns and flushing toilets. ENERGY STAR-approved ceiling fans, air conditioner, furnace, appliances, windows, and doors make the house efficient. Walls of thick and sturdy SIPs keep the house whisper-quiet and comfortable year-round.

A Clean Bill of Health

Heather grew up with asthma and allergies, so she was determined to build her house with materials that would not adversely affect her health. She selected materials and finishes that wouldn't off-gas toxic fumes, from an ever-expanding variety of products. Given a growing demand for healthier homes, many manufacturers now offer items that emit no or low VOCs.

BELOW Bathroom fixtures are low-flow and the toilet is an efficient dual-flush fixture, giving the user the option to flush with a small amount of water for liquid waste or a greater amount for solid waste.

OPPOSITE This upstairs bedroom is an example of how daylighting can illuminate rooms, minimizing dependency on artificial lights. PET carpeting in this room was made from recycled plastic bottles.

LEFT The openings for the glass blocks were cut out at the SIP plant before the blocks were installed on-site. The fireplace is a high-efficiency, sealed gas unit, used to supplement the heat on cold winter days.

BELOW The kitchen is energy efficient and environmentally friendly, from the ENERGY STAR appliances that minimize electricity use to the Formica countertops that, while seemingly old-fashioned, are quite eco-friendly.

Heather chose cabinets, paints, adhesives, and other materials that were made without toxic materials and thus avoid the resulting off-gassing of toxins into the home environment. Instead of the typical toxic options that contain formaldehyde and other chemicals, no-VOC stain was used on the wood cabinets and nontoxic cleaning supplies were provided for the final cleaning crew.

Concrete floors were scored, stained, and sealed rather than covered with dust-trapping carpet, which eventually would be replaced and dumped in a landfill. Drapery was kept at a minimum to prevent dust from collecting. Exhaust fans in the utility room and bathrooms help control moisture and prevent mold.

To control and prevent termite infestations, builders applied a non-chemical treatment during construction. A heavy vinyl barrier was created around the slab penetrations with a termiticide "locked in" between two layers.

A Real Investment

Many of the "green" qualities of Heather's house were accomplished with little or no investment. Orientation of the house relative to the seasonal movement of the sun in her location maximizes cross ventilation with the prevailing wind in warm months and passive solar heating in cold weather. Landscaping provides natural shading in the summer, when the trees are full of leaves, and solar gain in the winter, as the sun shines through the trees' bare limbs.

The Low-Tech Whole-House Fan

Whole-house fans draw cool evening air in through open windows and doors and exhaust warm air that has built up inside the house during the day. Years ago, attic fans performed a similar job, though not with the scientific energy-efficiency of today's whole-house fans. In Heather's Home the warm air is expelled out of the house through an awning window in the wall of her sealed, conditioned attic. This lowers indoor temperatures, extends the life of the roof, and reduces the need for air conditioning at a fraction of the cost. When the awning windows are closed in Heather's house, the attic is sealed; with the insulation provided by the SIPs, no conditioned air can escape out of the house. Fans in the attic can be activated manually or by timers. However, thermostats should not be used because they can run the fan when windows are closed or fires remain in the fireplace, potentially causing the fire to spread. Other drawbacks exist with whole-house fans. They suck in unfiltered air, bringing dust and pollen into the house. Fans also don't cool or dehumidify the air like air conditioners do. They must be sealed tightly and insulated to avoid losing conditioned air, or as in Heather's Home, fit inside a conditioned, insulated envelope with a window for the exhaust air.

BELOW The attic holds two whole-house fans, though only one is usually needed to evacuate hot air from the attic and roof.

BOTTOM A crane lifts the panels onto the foundation. Heather "hosted a 'barn raising' for the SIP installation and invited people to come and watch firsthand how they're installed," she said. (Photo supplied by Ferrier Custom Builders)

Below To protect the house from the southern sun, a standing seam metal Galvalume roof was installed. Metal roofs are long-lasting, durable, nearly maintenance-free, and reflect UV rays to help keep roofs and attics cool in the hot Texas summer. They're also recyclable. (Photo supplied by owner)

BOTTOM The rear view shows the overhangs that shield the house from the hot Texas sunshine in summer, but allow in the low winter sunlight, which helps the home gain heat.

Besides being exceptionally well-positioned for solar gain, Heather's house is also very well-insulated and tightly built. A typical house leaks so much air that it allows thirteen exchanges of air every hour (imagine your house breathing). Heather's house is so tight that it exchanges its air with outside air less than one time per hour. That might not provide enough air if you consider combustion appliances like water heaters and gas ranges, which use lots of air. To introduce more fresh air into Heather's house, an energy recovery ventilator (ERV) (see Heat and Energy Recovery Ventilation Systems sidebar, page 85) cycles fresh, filtered air into the house from outside for about five minutes every hour and recovers much of the heat or cooling from the interior air.

The house design also included careful plans to promote natural ventilation. Windows are plentiful and set to take best advantage of sun and breezes. The house is basically one-room deep, so air travels easily throughout the space. Overhangs on the rear windows and doors prevent the house from heating up during the hot Texas summers. Yet in the winter, the dense concrete floor absorbs solar energy coming in through the windows and radiates heat back into the house as the temperature falls during the night. These same floors, shaded from the sun in hot weather, stay cool and stabilize indoor temperatures at no cost.

When completed, the house cost $115 per square foot, which was at the high end of Heather's budget. But given that her utility bills are a third of what her neighbors in similar-sized houses pay each month, the initial cost was just part of the story. As Heather saw it, the green and energy-efficient elements of her house were more of an investment than a straight cost. Monthly heating and cooling costs, lower maintenance costs, and, ultimately, greater comfort balanced out construction costs to her satisfaction.

The mkLotus

Modular/SIPs

PHOTOGRAPHER:

John Swain Photographer,

(unless otherwise noted)

MANUFACTURER:

XtremeHomes

ARCHITECT:

Michelle Kaufmann Designs

LOCATION:

San Francisco, California

SIZE:

725 square feet

RATINGS:

GreenPoint Rated

LEED certification pending

GREEN ASPECTS

Solar-generated power

Green living roof

Sustainable layout for maximum cross ventilation and natural lighting

Rain and groundwater catchment system

Graywater system

FSC-certified wood: sheathing, siding, flooring, and cabinetry

Low-maintenance cement board siding

On-demand water heating

Energy-efficient HVAC system

Energy-efficient windows and doors

No-VOC paint

Concrete countertops made from fly ash, rice hull,

and recycled porcelain aggregates

Eco-friendly plumbing fixtures

LED lighting

ENERGY STAR appliances

Induction cooktop

Recycled glass and porcelain tiles

Interior doors comprised of 40 percent post-industrial

reclaimed material

Radiant heating

Spray foam insulation

Energy management home automation system

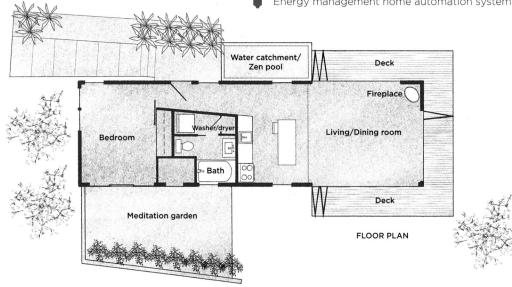

Water catchment/
Zen pool

Deck

Fireplace

Living/Dining room

Bedroom

Washer/dryer

Bath

Deck

Meditation garden

FLOOR PLAN

All the plants surrounding the house were chosen because they are regional, drought-tolerant, or functional, such as the bamboo, which is edible.

Michelle Kaufmann understands the meaning of *home*: comfort, shelter, protection. A space that reflects its occupants' sensitivity to energy and resource conservation. A cost-effective, uncomplicated building that lies cleanly on the earth.

She also understands that *home* can bring physical and spiritual renewal to the people inside. Unfortunately, many people who live in houses never know such a home. Michelle Kaufmann wants that to change.

Well known for her signature Sunset house, Michelle has emerged as an important young architect whose designs both look wonderful and work beautifully. Her mkLotus house underscores that growing reputation with its effective simplicity. mkLotus was built for West Coast Green, one of the nation's premier coming together of organizations committed to green building. The mkLotus is one of Michelle's greenest houses yet.

Basic Green

Every part of this house demonstrates the possibilities available in green construction. Solar panels on the roof produce 125 percent of its energy needs—needs that are kept to a miserly minimum thanks to elements like an on-demand, tankless water heater, energy-efficient HVAC system, LED lighting, and ENERGY STAR appliances. The technology carries even to the cooktop, an induction range that uses little energy, heats up only when the metal pan touches it, and stops radiating heat when the pan is taken away.

The house's design encourages cross ventilation with thoughtfully placed windows, skylight, and folding glass doors, which can open nearly the entire house up to the world outside, melding interior with exterior. Michelle says the house "*borrows* the sense of space from the landscape."

Large, full windows capture natural daylight, limiting the need for artificial lighting. The remote-controlled skylight shines light on all below, and also opens to create a chimney effect, drawing out unwanted heat on a warm day.

Nearly everything in the house is recycled or built with sustainable materials. The countertops and kitchen island are concrete mixed with rice hull and fly ash (a coal-fired power plant byproduct that adds strength and durability). The bathroom vanity uses the same concrete mixed with recycled porcelain, salvaged from tubs and sinks that would otherwise end in landfills. Recycled tiles cover the floor; 100 percent recycled glass tile decorates the walls.

For closet doors, Michelle used transparent resin panels to sandwich dried grass, literally bringing the surrounding nature indoors. The panels are chemical resistant, contain no hazardous materials, and include 40 percent postindustrial recycled material. For healthy interior air quality, builders used no-VOC paint, glue, chalks, and adhesives (paint colors were inspired by nature). Even the fireplace was chosen for its healthy operation and energy efficiency (see The EcoSmart Fireplace sidebar, opposite).

Michelle selected materials for durability

BELOW The mkLotus House is delivered to the site of the West Coast Green Show in San Francisco. (Photograph courtesy of Michelle Kaufmann Designs)

BOTTOM Snugly generating heat in the corner, the EcoSmart fireplace produces no smoke while warming as effectively as a wood-burning fireplace.

All About Light-Emitting Diodes

LED technology has been used for nearly fifty years to light digital clocks, electronic displays, and even televisions. But only recently, improvements in design and manufacturing made the technology a useful and green success. Chances are you'll soon see LEDs wherever you once saw only traditional lights. LEDs offer fine light, use less energy than conventional bulbs, and last up to 50,000 hours. They contain no mercury or lead, remain cool to the touch, won't cause fading, direct light better than other technologies, resist damage, and don't flicker. You'll find them in a variety of styles and shapes. Companies even manufacture waterproof LEDs for outdoor use. Although still more expensive than conventional lights, their efficiency and longevity are winning over consumers.

The EcoSmart Fireplace

Flueless and ventless, the EcoSmart fireplace burns clean ethanol-based alcohol and, much like our own breath, emits carbon dioxide and steam vapor instead of smoke and carbon dioxide. It is the only UL (Underwriters Classification) listed fireplace currently approved as flueless and ventless in California and New York. Extremely energy efficient, this fireplace puts out 13,000 BTUs, with no heat escaping up the chimney. Operating costs remain low at about $2 per hour. The fireplace can be used inside or out.

The GreenPoint Rated System

The nonprofit organization Build It Green trains and certifies raters, who are hired by builders or homeowners to evaluate, calculate and document the green elements going into a new home's construction. The rating system assesses energy and water efficiency, indoor air quality, material resource efficiency, and the greenness of the community itself, awarding points in every category, including for such items as proximity to mass transportation. The maximum score for GreenPoint Rated houses is around three hundred points, the minimum is fifty. Municipalities like San Jose and San Francisco mandate this minimum green standard for all houses over a certain size; for other counties, participation is voluntary. Visit www.builditgreen.org.

BELOW Recycled glass vodka bottle bases serve as a decorative element in the center of the water catchment basin.

RIGHT An angled view of the mkLotus house with the native garden and NANAWalls, a glass wall system, which opens up to expand the living space of the house.

Managing Graywater

Water from sinks, showers, bathtubs, and laundry traditionally goes into the sewer. A graywater management system redirects that water to flush toilets and irrigate lawns and gardens. Reusing graywater reduces stress on septic systems and treatment plants, can help promote plant growth, and, of real importance to the many drought-prone regions of the world, conserves water. If you are considering such a system, check local building codes for rules. You should also be conscious of the cleaning products that get into the system—nothing too harsh.

Modular Reduces Waste

Construction of a typical home generates around 8,000 pounds of debris. Scraps of wood, pipe, drywall, roofing, and flooring go into dumpsters and end up in landfills. Material is wasted; landfills are consumed. However, building in a modern factory, a builder can recycle the fewer scraps he generates into other projects or return them to the manufacturer for recycling. Manufacturers purchase materials in bulk, reducing the energy required to make many smaller deliveries to a construction site. Everything possible is ordered in the specific size necessary, and some companies even offer leftovers to the local community. Homeowners considering modular building should ask the manufacturer to explain their policies on recycling and describe the products they use in construction. Find out if they have green building experience and what extra costs come with meeting green standards.

Floors are recycled ceramic tile and walls are 55 percent recycled glass.

The bathroom sink has a low-flow fixture and concrete countertop made with fly ash and rice hull.

and sustainability. Floors and cabinets were made from FSC-certified wood from managed forests. The exterior decking is composite wood, combining low maintenance with extreme durability.

Sipping Water

Water conservation is one of Michelle's five "eco-principles" (which also include smart design, eco materials, energy efficiency, and healthy environment). In California, as in growing chunks of North America and the world, water—or not enough of it—is a massive concern. Several systems incorporated into mkLotus work hard to conserve the available water. A graywater system (see Managing Graywater sidebar, opposite) recycles water from the bath, sinks, and laundry. A rain and groundwater catchment system collects water for irrigation. The living roof insulates the house and leads water into the catchment basin for later use. Plumbing fixtures are low-flow, including a dual-flush toilet, which is estimated to save thousands of gallons a year.

The landscaping embodies all the same values as the house: conservation, recycling, and sensitivity to the environment. The surrounding land features plants native to the area that are drought-tolerant and in some cases practically functional, such as the living bamboo screen with edible shoots. Crushed up peach pits constitute the mulch; the paving around the house is recycled ceramic tile, tumbled to take off sharp edges; timbers were milled from salvaged city trees. The catch-basin water feature adds a functional as well as a decorative element to the landscape design.

Made to Grow

The mkLotus house has one bedroom, but variations include a two-bedroom as well as a two-story model. Tim Schmidt of manufacturer Xtreme-

Appliances are ENERGY STAR rated and the induction range heats up only in contact with metal, further conserving energy. Countertops are concrete mixed with recycled material.

RIGHT The cherry wood bed was made of FSC-certified wood finished only with oil and wax—no VOC emissions. The bedspread is one hundred percent flannel.

BELOW The closet door is not only eco-friendly but gives an open and airy appearance to this modestly sized room; the dried grass adds a natural dimension.

Homes worked closely with Michelle to create an energy-efficient house that can be mass-produced yet meet specific needs. Adaptations can be made for other climates. But you won't find any outrageous upgrade options. Michelle wants her houses available at a reasonable cost.

Besides being beautiful and sustainable, the mkLotus house is so highly efficient that it can produce enough energy to power the entire house *and* charge an electric car, which can plug into the side of the house to create a totally fuel-free lifestyle.

That's beautiful.

PowerHouse

Modular

PHOTOGRAPHER:

Eric Roth (unless otherwise noted)

ARCHITECT:

John D. Rossi, RA, LEED-AP

MANUFACTURER:

Epoch Homes

DEVELOPER:

PowerHouse Enterprises, Inc.

BUILDER:

NJZ Builders

LANDSCAPER:

Ould Towne Gardens

LOCATION:

Lawrence, Massachusetts

SIZE:

1,468 square feet

RATINGS:

LEED-H—Platinum

GREEN ASPECTS:

Infill lot

Passive solar orientation

Precast insulated foundation

High-efficiency HVAC system

ENERGY STAR programmable thermostat

ENERGY STAR appliances

ENERGY STAR ceiling fans

Low-VOC finishes and paints

Pergola incorporating recycled shipping pallets

Dual-flush toilets

Low-flow showerheads

FSC-certified wood

Energy recovery ventilation system

Low-wattage halogen and CFL bulbs

Aluminum-clad windows

Galvalume metal siding

Locally sourced recycled wood flooring

High-efficiency windows/aluminum and wood frames

Spray foam insulation

Engineered wood siding

Recycled content drywall

Recycled content carpeting

Programmable thermostats

Pebble driveway for drainage

FIRST FLOOR

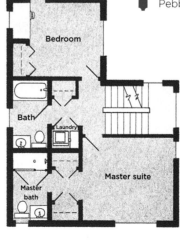

SECOND FLOOR

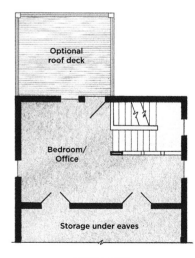

THIRD FLOOR

The house blends in with the older neighboring houses and commercial facilities in design and materials. The pergola over the front entrance includes lumber recycled from shipping pallets that were used to send construction materials to the site. All packaging and leftover materials that could be used were recycled.

awrence, Massachusetts, has a reputation as a down-on-its-luck former mill town 30 miles northwest of Boston. Poorer by far than its big sister on the bay, Lawrence isn't the type of place where you'd expect to find much innovation, let alone a breakthrough in green building.

But it's also not the type of place to throw up its hands and surrender to the forces of decline. So when the city auctioned off an empty residential lot in town, it added a provision: Whoever won the lot and built a house had to make it LEED certifiable.

The city received plenty of bids, but picked one of the low ones—an $11,000 offer from a company called PowerHouse. In return, Quincy Vale, the president of PowerHouse, and his architect, John Rossi, decided to go beyond the city's demands. The house they built would be LEED certifiable and green through and through; it would also be outfitted with the latest technology and designed not just as a place to live in, but as a place to enjoy. On top of all that, the house would be *affordable*—not a word typically connected with "green building."

The PowerHouse project appealed to the city leaders, who were undertaking the city's most recent effort at revitalizing the old mill town and recapturing some of its lost glory (it was the first planned industrial community in the country as well as the place where Robert Frost wrote his first poem). Their plans dovetailed well with the PowerHouse philosophy. The new green house on Market Street would set an example and send the message that the world was changing and that Lawrence was paying attention.

The Heart of Green Building

Basic green building principles include resource conservation, energy efficiency, and reducing environmental impact. Few methods of building more closely match those principles than prefab. When it comes to prefabrication, Quincy is a believer. He goes so far as to say that ". . . a house cannot be very green unless it's modular or some type of prefab, since those . . . systems reduce waste and lead to much higher quality control . . ."

The house on Market Street would be prefab. And it would sit atop a prefab foundation (nearly all foundations are poured in place). Most elements of house construction can be made better and more efficiently in controlled conditions, Quincy believes. Poured foundations take about four weeks to cure. The PowerHouse foundation was precision-crafted in a mold, cured under factory-controlled conditions, and was strong and ready for the house on the day of installation. The foundation also arrived on site insulated and prefinished inside.

Quincy and his builder, James Passios, picked Epoch homes to craft the custom modular components in its plant in next-door New Hampshire. Working as a team, the group figured out how to modify the process to ensure that the house got its "LEED for Homes" platinum certification— the Nobel prize of green building. All adhesives,

LEFT A crane lifts the precast insulated foundation into place, completing the job in under two hours. (Photo by John Rossi)

LEFT A crane lifts the precast insulated foundation into place, completing the job in under two hours. (Photo by John Rossi)

BELOW The last of the home's four modules is set in place, where it will be "married" to the other sections to create a nearly seamless whole. (Photo by John Rossi)

All the carpeting on the second and third floors is made from
recycled fibers.

BELOW The uppermost level was designed as a playroom or office.
When the windows are open, warm air rising up from below
vents outside.

BOTTOM Modest but highly appealing, the kitchen includes all
ENERGY STAR-rated appliances. Large swing-out casement windows
flood the kitchen and dining area with natural sunlight.

Reducing VOCs

Paint, clear finishes, adhesives—even many cleaning supplies—contain volatile organic compounds (VOCs) that slowly release toxic gas into the home. Health risks from breathing VOCs can include eye, nose, and throat irritation as well as liver, kidney, and central nervous system damage. Recently, most paint companies began replacing VOCs with newer and safer ingredients. Look for interior paint certified with a Green Seal™ rating for VOC content less than 50 grams per liter (g/l) for flat paint or 150 g/l for other finishes. Products that meet Canada's VOC standards carry their EcoLogo (a green maple leaf intertwined with three doves). To learn more, check www.epa.gov/iaq/voc.html.

Programmable Thermostats

Programmable thermostats provide the option to set the temperature for a variety of schedules, such as turning down the heat at bedtime and turning it back up before your alarm clock rings. Set it; forget it; save energy and money. A programmable thermostat can reduce 1,847 pounds of green house gas emissions per year and save you about $187 a year in heating and cooling costs. For additional information, check www.energystar.gov/programablethermostats.

primers, and finishes were low-VOC. PowerHouse insulated with Icynene, (see Spray Foam Insulation sidebar, page 75) an expanding spray-foam insulation that offers very high R-values as well as seals up walls to stop energy-robbing air leaks.

All the wood in the house was sustainably harvested and certified by the Forest Steward Council. Windows were carefully specified to maximize energy efficiency, balanced with appearance and durability, at a reasonable cost. The four prefab modules that became the PowerHouse were set in a day and made weathertight.

The Invisible Green

In his design, John applied a principle he calls "invisible green." The house would not look strange or unusual; it wouldn't stick out in the neighborhood as some out-of-place oddity, but it would certainly be green. One would have to look hard to notice signs of its remarkable energy and resource efficiency.

9 foot ceilings and big windows limit the need for expensive artificial light and ventilation. Heated air rises in the winter and a ceiling fan gently sends it back down to floor level. In the summer, the three-story staircase is allowed to function like a chimney, drawing hot air up and out through large third-floor windows. For cross ventilation, windows were installed on as many sides of a room as possible. Awning windows paired with casement windows on the first and second floors let cool breezes flow through the house even when it's raining.

These "invisible" features keep the house cool and comfortable without air conditioning. The design strategy also minimized wasted space like hallways, which take away from living areas. With just 7 feet of hallway (or only 3 percent of the total living space as opposed to up to 15 percent hallway space in conventional houses),

nearly every inch of the PowerHouse is used for living. And fewer and smaller halls mean fewer unnecessary walls, which minimizes material and construction costs and reduces heating and cooling.

Looking into the Future

John's top priority was to create a comfortable and beautiful environment in a sustainable and cost-effective manner for present and future occupants, a goal that he and the team accomplished beautifully. Wherever possible, he chose materials and components that were either recycled, recyclable, or both. The pergola over the front entrance was built of wood shipping pallets. The vertical metal siding that covers part of the house is highly recyclable (and also reflects the look of nearby warehouses and mills in the area).

All materials used in the windows—glass, wood, and aluminum—are recycled or recyclable. The rustic flooring throughout the first floor was salvaged from the old Duck Mill building three blocks away. Though not inexpensive, it was "mostly an aesthetic choice," according to John, who says building affordably doesn't mean that everything is low cost. Given the opportunity to save money at all costs or spend a little more for something with character, the architect showed that "green," affordable, and beautiful can be balanced.

A single high-efficiency boiler sends warm water to individual zones throughout the house, both for heating and for hot water. An advanced monitoring system, using a series of sensors around the house, tracks heat and moisture levels to reduce or increase heat and ventilation as necessary. At current rates, the home's energy efficiency will save the owner $2,500 per year, even compared to other new homes at current local energy code standards. Homeowners will

An ENERGY STAR-rated ceiling fan helps keep the house cool in hot weather. In winter, the fan is reversed and softly moves warm air off the ceiling and down to people below.

BELOW Shipping pallets used to send construction materials to the site became part of the pergola over the front entrance. Everything that could be used was recycled.

RIGHT The front entrance is colorful and bright; a warm welcome into this cheerful house.

BELOW RIGHT The deck offers a connection to the outdoors, especially imprtant in its tight urban infill location.

Faucets are all low-flow and the toilet is dual-flush to help restrict water use and lower operating costs of the house.

also save $450 annually in sewer and water fees alone, compared to traditional houses in the area. Dual-flush toilets (see Dual-Flush Toilets sidebar, page 148), low-flow showerheads, and a high-efficiency dishwasher make a substantial impact in daily water usage.

Way up on the south-facing roof, John and Quincy created a wide shed dormer that floods the third-floor bedroom/office with sunlight. However, the dormer accomplishes more than simply increasing headroom and natural light. The angle, or pitch, of the dormer roof was precisely calculated to ensure optimum exposure to the sun. If the homeowners of this house ever decide to change their energy source, that roof will perfectly accommodate solar panels.

Making the City Proud

When the house was complete, a celebration and open house were held—on a day when temperatures barely rose above zero. The mayor of Lawrence and hundreds of visitors came to tour the house and celebrate some good news and positive change in their city.

The PowerHouse model set an example and opened the door to moderately priced green construction in Lawrence and in other struggling cities throughout the country.

Excellent planning and thoughtful use of materials and systems resulted in a house that is more than extremely energy efficient and built of the most sustainable materials. The house has charm and appeal; it's a house anyone would enjoy calling home.

LEAFHouse

Modular

PHOTOGRAPHER:

Jim Tetro (unless otherwise noted)

BUILDER:

University of Maryland

LOCATION:

National Mall, Washington, D.C.

SIZE:

800 square feet

GREEN ASPECTS:

Indoor liquid desiccant waterfall for dehumidification

Passive solar

PV panels

Solar water heating system

Ductless cooling

Drain water heat recovery system

Storm water management system

Graywater system

Green wall

Locally harvested wood

FSC-Certified wood for framing and finish

Recycled corrugated metal siding

Soy-based spray foam insulation

Smart house system

Radiant floor heating

ENERGY STAR appliances

Induction cooktop

Renewable and recycled materials

Combination washer-dryer

Dual-flush toilet

Fluorescent and LED lighting

Energy recovery ventilator

Low-VOC paint

FSC-Certified eastern white pine

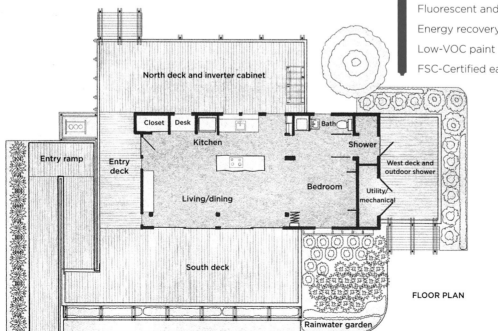

FLOOR PLAN

Inspired by a leaf, which converts sunlight into useful energy, the
LEAFHouse motto—"Leading Everyone to an Abundant Future"—also
denotes the hope of the students who designed and built the house.
Not just aesthetically pleasing, the house functioned for ten days at
the Solar Decathlon, creating all of its own energy and then some.
(Photograph by Amy E. Gardner)

In green design, symbolism is sometimes as important as substance. In the LEAF-House, designed and built by students at the University of Maryland, symbol and substance became one.

The three goals of the team were straightforward: to advance sustainable design and construction, to use nature as inspiration for design, and to demonstrate that solar technology is practical for everyday life.

LEAFHouse was designed and built using the best of traditional knowledge about construction married with new and innovative technologies, and utilizing readily available materials in creative and innovative ways. The signature example of this approach is the central "stem" of skylights that run the length of the house. Constructed from FSC-certified wood, ordinary structural steel, and a polycarbonate skylight system, the roof provides an integrated solution in which structure, thermal performance, and daylighting strategies come together.

This prototype house was built at the university and transported to the Mall in Washington, D.C., for the Solar Decathlon in 2007. The University is planning on working with a modular company to develop a version of LEAFHouse to market to consumers.

Machine for Living

The house is strikingly attractive and well proportioned. But the team needed it to do more that look good. The design had to perform all the necessary functions of an ordinary house—such as heating, cooling, lighting, and making hot water—as well as accomplish the simply stated but difficult to achieve goal of becoming a good home for the eventual inhabitants. The systems also had to adapt to the homeowners' needs and be easy to operate.

Two engineering students developed the Smart House Adaptive Control (SHAC), an automated control system with web-linked intelligence that could track current weather and solar conditions and direct the house to optimize energy use, humidity, light, and water consumption. The system collects data around the house, monitors conditions, and performs tasks to efficiently and economically manage the home as required to create a comfortable environment.

Some of these smart house functions include monitoring and controlling the lighting and liquid desiccant waterfall systems. LEAFHouse's smart house SHAC system also continually evaluates interior lighting levels and responds to the natural light outdoors by balancing electric with natural light. The system helps control energy use and improve the environment for inhabitants. Homeowners can control dimming levels according to who's home, the time of day, and the type of activity. SHAC also can advise the homeowner to conserve energy if the extended weather report calls for clouds (solar panels don't like clouds).

One unique feature of the house is the liquid desiccant dehumidifier, which removes moisture

PREVIOUS PAGE Plentiful windows and aero-gel-filled polycarbonate skylights provide views to the surrounding landscape and abundant daylight. All appliances in the kitchen are ENERY STAR-rated. The dining table, made of the same sustainably forested veneer as the frames around the big sliding doors, can be transformed into two full tables, each seating six. The kitchen island includes a concrete countertop that contains 6 percent recycled fly ash and 30 percent recycled glass. The maple sections were salvaged from naturally fallen trees in nearby Thurmont.

LEFT A series of moveable translucent panels transform various areas of the house to provide efficient use of space. The bedroom on the right can be opened up and the Murphy bed closed to create space for entertaining. Glass tiles in the shower are made from recycled glass.

Walls on two sides of the bedroom can be closed off with translucent polycarbonate panels for privacy or opened to expand the entertaining area. The Murphy bed, as well as other furnishings in the house, can be integrated into the walls to increase available space.

from the air while also serving as an aesthetic waterfall element.

Going Gridless

Although the LEAFHouse was hooked up to the grid when it returned to the university, on the Mall it functioned entirely as a solar-powered house, without any city electricity.

The thirty-four solar panels on the roof provided power for all electrical needs. The forty-eight 12-volt batteries could store enough energy when the sun shone to power everything in the house for up to four days. The north/south orientation of the house, with the preponderance of natural light pouring in from clerestory windows that run the length of the structure and from the large glass doors and windows on the south side of the house, works to minimize artificial light needs.

Low-energy LED and fluorescent lighting controlled by a "smart" lighting system and ENERGY STAR appliances helped to further decrease the energy usage. Spray foam insulation kept the envelope of the house well padded to minimize the need for heating and cooling, saving even more energy.

Transformability

The house was built to adapt to all seasons and to the changing needs of day-to-day life.

With the Murphy bed stowed out of sight, translucent panels surrounding the bedroom open to transform a private space into an entertaining area. Large sliding glass doors open to the deck, effortlessly blending indoor with outdoor space. Louvers were designed to allow the light to enter in the winter and be deflected in the warm months.

The LEAFHouse is back on the University of Maryland campus, set onto a permanent foundation, where it will serve as the office and meeting place for the Potomac Valley Chapter of the American Institute of Architects. There it will continue to educate and inspire.

OPPOSITE ABOVE One striking element of the house is the double roof with a racking system that provides housing for the photovoltaic (PV) panels that supply all the house's energy. The double roof encourages airflow between the upper panels and the lower roof, thereby cooling the house as well as the back of the panels. The roof has solar panels as well as PV panels.

OPPOSITE BELOW This vertical garden on the south side of the house serves not only as an aesthetic element but also functions as part of the storm water management system. It filters the runoff water from the roof and irrigates the adjacent garden.

BELOW University of Maryland students load the LEAFHouse onto a flatbed truck for transporting it to the National Mall, which took three hours. The team spent two days assembling the solar racking system and attaching the solar panels and five more days reassembling the house and landscape elements. (Photograph by Amy E. Gardner)

Solar Decathlon

Every two years on the National Mall in Washington, D.C. teams of college students build houses of their own design. And not just any houses: solar-powered ones. Sponsored by the United States Department of Energy's Office of Energy Efficiency and Renewable Energy and the National Renewable Energy Laboratory, the event draws students from the United States, Puerto Rico, Canada, and Europe, who compete in ten categories including architecture, engineering, market viability, comfort, lighting, and energy balance. The demands require a sophisticated design. The teams must do more than build the houses. They have to prove that they function. Students demonstrate that solar power will cook meals, provide heat and air conditioning, and heat water for showers and washing clothes in the washing machine. And the electric cars provided to each team must be powered by solar energy generated by the team's house. Additional points accumulate based on how many miles each team can drive on their energy. The LEAFHouse by the University of Maryland team came in second place overall in the 2007 competition, behind a house built by students from Germany. Each team comprises a multitude of disciplines under the direction of faculty advisers and outside trade mentors. The goal is to construct innovative houses that use only solar energy. For more on the Solar Decathlon, visit www.solardecathlon.org. To learn more about the University of Maryland's LEAFHouse, visit www.solarteam.org.

Highland House

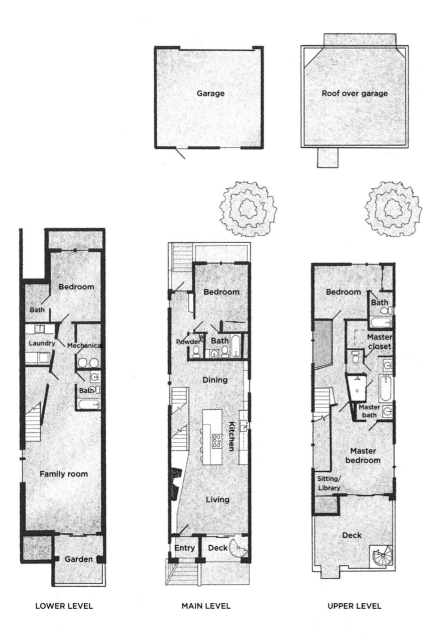

LOWER LEVEL

Bedroom
Bath
Laundry
Mechanical
Bath
Family room
Garden

MAIN LEVEL

Bedroom
Powder
Bath
Dining
Kitchen
Living
Entry
Deck

UPPER LEVEL

Bedroom
Bath
Master closet
Master bath
Sitting/Library
Master bedroom
Deck

Garage

Roof over garage

Modular

PHOTOGRAPHER:

Ben Tremper (unless otherwise noted)

ARCHITECT:

Brad Tomecek, Studio H:T

MANUFACTURER:

Barvista Homes

BUILDER:

John Cianci, Eco-Infill

LOCATION:

Denver, Colorado

SIZE:

2,700 square feet

RATINGS:

LEED-H—Silver

GREEN ASPECTS:

Infill site

Brick reconstructed

Passive solar design

Community location

ENERGY STAR appliances

ENERGY STAR windows

92.5 percent efficient furnace

Bamboo flooring

Recycled rubber paver tiles

Recycled composite decking

Low-VOC paints

Drought-resistant landscaping

High-performance fireplace

The exterior is composed of both
stucco and fiber cement siding.
Landscaping was kept to a minimum
using rock, which helps retain soil per-
meability for storm water absorption,
accented with drought-resistant plants.

The lot was in the middle of a "transitional neighborhood," better known as the other side of the tracks, and only 25 feet wide, hardly big enough for a trailer home.

Yet architect Brad Tomecek saw its potential. Just a short distance from downtown Denver, the Highland neighborhood has become a "sweet spot" on the edge of downtown. Because of the neighborhood's affordability and proximity, Brad can bike from his home to parks and restaurants, not easily done in the ranging suburbs that ring the Mile High city.

Saving What's Salvageable

A neglected 600 square-foot house with an unstable foundation occupied the lot when Brad found it. He says the house was more than run-down; it was the "ugliest house on the block."

He decided he had to tear the house down, rather than try to rebuild it. In his desire to make the future house on the property as green as possible, he had the demolition company salvage the old brick from the façade. He donated the brick to them, and they cleaned it up to resell it.

Going with Modular

As an architect, Brad had designed houses using a variety of building systems, from structural insulated panels to recycled shipping containers. And he was up to date on the newest green products and technologies.

This was his first project, however, that he planned to have certified as green. He hoped to build the house using "accessible," or off-the-shelf green products, to employ conventional building techniques executed in a factory at a high level of quality, and to build the whole thing at a price that would compete with a conventionally built structure. Modular construction seemed perfect for his needs.

Due to the narrow lot, the local zoning regulations specified that any house could not measure more than 19 feet wide. The modular company Brad had in mind could build the house to 18 feet wide, allowing leeway for siding and trim. It took just over five months to complete the house from the time the first shovel of dirt was turned for the foundation. It took four hours to set the house.

Without a six-week delay caused by a utility company (which shut the job down), the house would have been complete in a mere four months. A house built on-site usually takes at least twice that time.

A large percentage of the house was complete on delivery. The modules had windows and doors as well as much of the interior finishes, such as bamboo floors, bath and kitchen cabinets, and some lighting and plumbing fixtures. The builders, Eco-Infill, completed some exterior items on site, such as the rubber membrane (EPDM) roof system, stucco and fiber cement siding, and such interior features as countertops and specialty lighting.

The modular manufacturer, Barvista Homes, agreed to accommodate most of the green

An employee at Studio H:T, Justin Ewing, produced and gifted the painting over the fireplace. The direct vent gas fireplace gives off good heat to the room. The niche beside the fireplace was built in the factory and adds visual interest to that area of the house.

features Brad specified for the house, including the type of insulation and energy-efficient windows. Some items—a high-efficiency furnace, for example—were not a standard item for the company. Brad purchased the furnace himself and had it installed on-site.

Many modular companies like Barvista are responding to the growing demand for greener houses and have begun to make these items more accessible in the houses they build.

Making It Official

Brad's house received many points towards LEED certification by virtue of the location and its proximity to neighborhood amenities. Other points accrued through using passive measures such as orientation of the house with the sun and construction of an airtight envelope.

With a tight exterior including windows and doors and energy-efficient appliances and systems, the cost of heating and cooling the house is about the same as that of Brad's old house, which was 50 percent bigger than this one. The Highland House received a silver rating even without such active measures as photovoltaics and solar hot water systems.

The project garnered a variety of awards, including *Builder Magazine's* Builder's Choice Award for 2008 and the local chapter of the American Institute of Architects' (AIA) Merit Award.

ABOVE The master bedroom on the upper level is flooded with light from the large doors and narrow windows, which also provide privacy.

ABOVE RIGHT The structure's two modules were carefully lifted into place on this narrow, 25-foot lot. In the morning, only a foundation existed; four hours later, an almost complete house sat on the property. (Photo by owner)

OPPOSITE ABOVE The kitchen cabinets and bamboo floors were all installed in the factory. Appliances are ENERGY STAR-rated.

OPPOSITE BELOW A local artist, Michael Warren, painted the series over the couch. The large sliding door floods the living room with light while translucent shades allow in light and secure privacy.

Bamboo Flooring

When bamboo is harvested for flooring or countertops, new bamboo quickly replaces it. The fast-growing grass (it really is a form of grass!) has increased in popularity as a renewable resource, as it can be harvested every three to six years, depending on where it's planted. In Asia, bamboo has been used as a building material since the dawn of civilization. Relatively new to North American builders, bamboo has become an attractive alternative to traditional hardwoods because of its beauty, durability, and environmental sustainability. Of its many species, the one most often used for flooring is moso, which can grow to a height of 80 feet and a diameter of 6 inches. Once harvested, the bamboo is split lengthwise to extract the premium part of the stalk, flattened into 3/4-inch strips, and laminated under high pressure to produce flooring sections. These are usually kiln-dried and treated with a natural borate solution to eliminate the sugar and starches that attract pests. Before purchasing bamboo flooring or furnishing, consumers with allergies or sensitivity to certain products should check to see what adhesives and finishing products were used in the production.

What's Old Is Green Again

Usually, when a house is torn down, everything ends up in a landfill. In recent years, however, people have become more conscious of waste and more attuned to the architectural treasures that can be recycled from an older home. Homeowners and builders routinely reuse materials such as metal roofing and siding—now they also salvage bricks, tile, paneling, fixtures, windows, doors, and even beams from older houses. While reducing the amount of waste that goes into the landfill, these builders often gain irreplaceable elements from the past. In the Highland House, the bricks removed from the previous house on the lot were stored and donated to a demolition company that cleaned and resold them. Many organizations now exist that deconstruct old houses slated for demolition, removing any valuable items for resale. Habitat for Humanity performs this service and offers Re-Stores throughout the country to sell recycled house parts. To learn more, visit www.habitat.org.

BELOW Local artist Hyland Mathers created the artwork on the wall. A friend of Brad's who is a local steel artist, built the steel-frame table with a Baltic birch top.

OPPOSITE A rooftop deck outside the master bedroom beckons for Saturday morning reading and relaxation. The beautiful view includes Coors Field, where the Colorado Rockies play, and the steeple of an old church on the opposite corner.

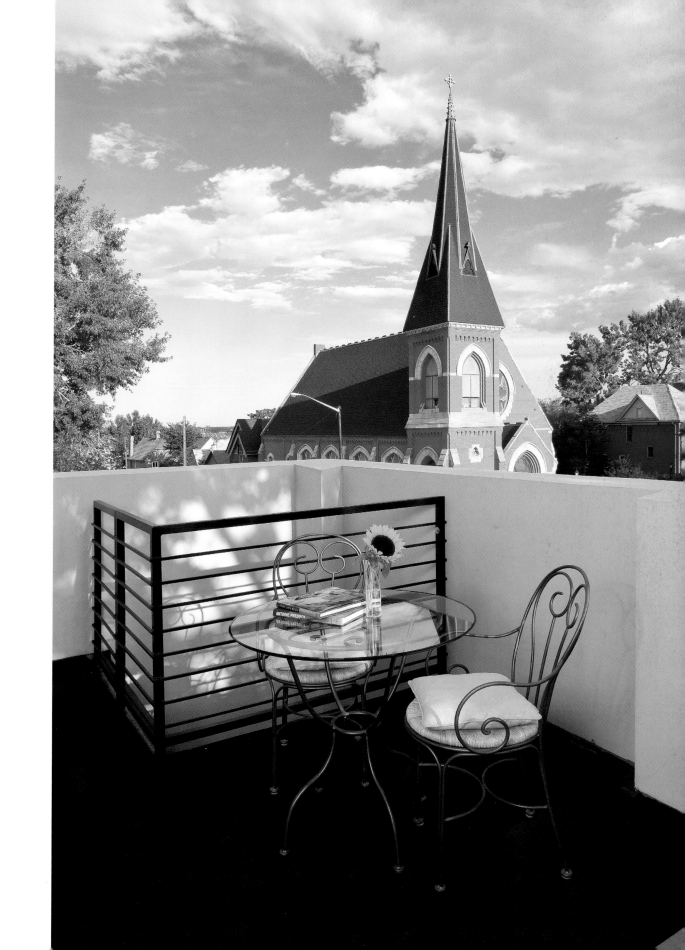

LivingHome

Modular/Steel frame

ARCHITECT:

Ray Kappe

MANUFACTURER:

LivingHomes

LOCATION:

Santa Monica, California

SIZE:

4,057 square feet

RATINGS:

LEED-H—Platinum

ENERGY STAR

GREEN ASPECTS:

Photovoltaic system

Solar water heating

Radiant heating system

ENERGY STAR appliances

Recycled paper countertops

Recycled glass tiles

LED lighting

Low-VOC paints and finishes

Water-efficient bathroom fixtures

Recycled glass countertops

All FSC-certified Wood

Recycled denim insulation

Graywater system

Rainwater catchment system

Whole-house fan

Indoor garden

Native landscape

Green roof

Previous house on lot deconstructed

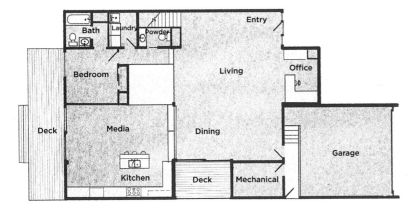

FIRST FLOOR

SECOND FLOOR

Just how would you go about designing and building a green house if you had no standards or guidelines to follow?

Until 2005, when the U.S. Green Building Council (USGBC) established a pilot program called Leadership in Energy and Environmental Design (now famously known as LEED), architects and builders—not to mention consumers— had no comprehensive vision of what makes a house eco-friendly. But when those early guidelines came out, Steve Glenn was determined to use them in building the first LEED Certified Platinum house in the United States.

Using the entrepreneurial expertise he'd accumulated through years of working with socially conscious nonprofits and technology startups, Steve created LivingHomes, a company with a goal to build the greenest and healthiest homes in the country. These houses would have the least impact on the environment and sell at a more affordable price than similarly sized site-built custom homes.

To design the first group of LivingHomes, Steve called on his favorite architect, Ray Kappe, known for designing California modernist homes that are prefabricated, earth-friendly, site sensitive, and extremely livable. They began seeking out recycled and recyclable materials and healthy systems that could make a house self-sufficient for energy and water, and could adapt to meet the occupants' changing lifestyles.

Steve especially wanted his first LEED home to serve as a model for future green houses: Zero energy, zero water, zero waste, zero carbon, zero emissions; what's called a *net zero* house. The first home would be his own and would serve as the model home for his company.

Building the Green Dream

The home was a steel-and-glass modular, constructed in a local factory where it generated 75 percent less waste than a typical site-built house. In April 2006, in an eight-hour day, a 350-ton crane set the eleven modules onto a concrete slab, erecting the first of many eventual LivingHomes.

Three months after the crane set the house, Steve moved in. He had pulled out all the stops for his house; it would set a high standard for others to follow. It would be the first and foremost LEED Platinum home in the country.

Steve designed all the materials and systems to limit impact on the environment. Water for domestic use (bathing, drinking, and washing) and for the radiant floor heating system uses solar heat. The radiant floor system warms efficiently and, unlike forced hot air, it does not move dust and other contaminants throughout a house. Photovoltaic panels on the roof meet the home's energy requirements as well as shading the rooftop. The appliances are ENERGY STAR-rated and the lights are LED, which use a fraction of the energy required by incandescent lights. The house operates 80 percent more efficiently than a conventional residence of similar size, which also qualifies it as ENERGY STAR-rated.

BELOW AND PREVIOUS PAGE Front trellises deflect sun, keeping the house cooler and conserving energy. All deck wood is FSC-certified tigerwood, a very dense South American hardwood that is smooth and splinter-free. Siding is a beautiful FSC-certified cedar, which is extremely weather resistant. (Photo by Tom Bonner)

ABOVE The indoor garden includes some plants that produce oxygen and others that filter the air of contaminants. The concrete floor is reinforced with fly ash, a material recycled from coal combustion in electric generating plants. (Photo by Berg/Divis)

LEFT All appliances are ENERGY STAR-rated, fixtures are water efficient, and the kitchen countertop is made of 100 percent post-consumer recycled newspaper—both beautiful and extremely strong. (Photo by Berg/Divis)

70 percent of the exterior walls are high-efficiency glass with three times the thermal properties of ordinary glass. During the day, the concrete floors absorb the sunlight that pours in through the walls of glass; they slowly radiate the heat back into the home overnight. Strategically located trellises deflect the sun in the warmer months while casting beautiful shadows in the afternoon.

Besides being a beautiful and restful retreat, the rooftop garden also helps insulate the roof, lessening the need for mechanical heating. A whole-house fan brings cool air into the house when needed and removes warm air as necessary, eliminating air conditioning requirements.

Serious Conservation

Landscaper Richard Grigsby's system requires no city water. The city of Santa Monica, which encourages water reclamation and conservation, provided a grant for the system. Water recycled from sinks and showers (called gray water) irrigates the front yard. Elsewhere, the property slopes too much to use gray water, which could run off onto neighboring property. A storm water management system collects rainwater in a cistern to irrigate those parts of the lot.

Both elements use a buried drip system that prevents water from pooling, which can allow fungus and other plant diseases to develop. Both systems depend on gravity to carry water into an irrigation tank. Richard says these methods currently cost more than traditional irrigation systems, but that the price will decrease as they become more common and more readily available.

Further water is conserved in the house with the use of water-efficient fixtures and dual-flush toilets throughout.

Good Home Health

The LivingHome features formaldehyde- and urea-free millwork and surfaces finished with either no-VOC or low-VOC paint (see Reducing VOCs sidebar, page 177). Exhaust fans in bathrooms reduce moisture, eliminating the chance of mold and mildew. To decrease the possibility of carbon monoxide exhaust entering the living space, an exhaust fan vents straight outside from the garage.

Inside, Richard designed a garden that incorporates plants that, according to information taken from a NASA report*, actually scrub the air of harmful gases like benzene, formaldehyde, and trichloroethylene. The toxin-fighting plant selection includes varieties of *Philodendrons, Dracaena, Ficus benjamina* (weeping fig), *Epipremnum aureum* (golden pathos), and *Spathiphyllum* mauna loa (peace lily)—all of which are both functional and attractive.

Throughout the house, Steve incorporated recycled and sustainable materials. For instance, all wood, including the tigerwood decks and cedar siding, is FSC (Forest Stewardship Council) certified (see What FSC Is All About sidebar, page 102), which means all wood comes from responsibly sustained forests. Whenever possible, he used materials salvaged from other projects. Countertops are made from 100 percent post-consumer material, the glass walls are made from recycled glass, and even the insulation was made from 100 percent pre-consumer garment mill waste—in this case, blue jeans (see Recycled Denim Insulation sidebar, opposite).

Interior Landscape Plants for Indoor Air Pollution Abatement, September 1989, by Dr. B.C. Wolverton, Anne Johnson, and Keith Bounds, National Aeronautics and Space Administration, John C. Stennis Space Center, Stennis Space Center, MS 39529-6000.

Built for Change

To Steve, simply building a house that meets very high environmental standards wasn't enough. For the house to truly be sustainable—to serve its inhabitants well for many years to come with minimal use of resources—it would also need to be adaptable. Steve needs the house to work for him, but he knows that a future generation living there will likely have different lifestyle requirements. The LivingHome needed to keep up.

Remodeling is a disruptive, messy business. Steve wanted to ensure that future dwellers in his house could make necessary changes simply. He incorporated several features in the design to simplify that process.

He designed the walls to be moveable. Millwork is modular, or "plugged in," so it can be easily relocated. And the home's structural system allows rooms to be added or shifted.

Steve has since sold several of the homes to other families, each with small variations. By standardizing the design and selling houses in volume, the company can now produce these homes on a sort of factory assembly line, buying materials in bulk and using standard and interchangeable parts to further reduce waste and costs.

LEFT Recycled denim insulation. (Photo courtesy of Bonded Logic, Inc.)

OPPOSITE The resin panels in the bathroom are made of 40 percent nontoxic recycled plastic. The embedded plant material gives the panels a clean, natural look. Countertops are recycled cement strengthened with cellulose fibers; bath tiles are recycled porcelain. Fluorescent lights provide great light with less energy; faucets are low-flow and toilets are dual-flush to reduce water use. (Photograph by Tom Bonner)

LEED Certified

The U.S. Green Building Council created the LEED for Homes rating system to promote high-performance green design and construction. The goal is a nation of houses that use less energy and fewer resources, produce less waste, and have healthier and more comfortable interior environments. LEED homes qualify at four levels: Certified, Silver, Gold, and Platinum, based on points earned in a variety of categories. Reaching one of these levels requires commitment. Accredited providers work with homeowners, architects, and builders to assist through the design and construction process and submit the final LEED checklist to the USGBC for certification. Some LEED measures are optional; others are mandatory. Also, a house must achieve a minimum score on the Home Energy Rating System (HERS) index, a number determined by a blower door test (see The Blower Door Test sidebar, page 126) and a test that measures the leakiness of the ductwork. Steve's house was the first house in the country to achieve LEED Platinum, with 91 points out of a possible 108. To learn more, visit www.greenhomeguide.org or www.usgbc.org.

Recycled Denim Insulation

As a nation, we love our blue jeans. Thankfully, the waste produced by blue jean manufacturers is waste no more. Rather than incinerating denim scraps or dumping them into landfills, blue jean makers are turning leftover denim into useful insulation that not only holds in heat (with an R-value of R-13 to R-30), and reduces sound transmission; the insulation is also non-irritating, VOC-free, resistant to mold, fungi, and bacteria, and, thanks to a natural borate treatment, merits a Class A fire rating. Denim insulation is available as batts (8 feet by 16 or 24 inches) and is 100 percent recyclable. To learn more, visit www.bondedlogic.com.

Paper Countertops

Paper-based countertops offer a terrific alternative to stone and other traditional materials. Two companies now offer such products: PaperStone, used in Steve's house, makes three products. One uses 100 percent post-consumer recycled cardboard; another FSC-certified product is made from 100 percent recycled office paper; and virgin fibers constitute the third option. PaperStone binds their products with a petroleum-free resin and uses natural ingredients, including cashew shell nut oil and organic pigments. Countertops and other items (such as windowsills and door thresholds) made of PaperStone are scratch resistant and have uniform color throughout, so no substrate shows even if the material does get scratched. The products are impervious to water, stain resistant, carry a Class A fire rating, and come with a fifteen year limited warranty. Another company offering paper countertops is Richlite. To learn more, visit www.paperstone.com or www.richlite.com.

BELOW Cork floors are warm, comfortable, renewable, and resistant to mold, mildew, and fire. The ceiling is made of FSC-certified cedar. A screen of recycled plastic lowers to filter sunlight, increasing energy efficiency and privacy while still providing a view outside. (Photo by Berg/Divis)

BOTTOM Media room (Photo by Berg/Divis)

OPPOSITE The open floor plan gives this house a very open and spacious feel. (Photo by Berg/Divis)

Back from the Burn

Modular

PHOTOGRAPHER:

Carolyn Bates (unless otherwise noted)

ARCHITECT/BUILDER:

John Connell, 2Morrow Studio

MANUFACTURER:

Customized Structures, Inc. (CSI)

LOCATION:

South Burlington, Vermont

SIZE:

1,834 square feet (not including basement)

RATINGS:

ENERGY STAR—5 stars

LEED-H–certified

GREEN ASPECTS:

FSC-certified wood

Locally harvested and manufactured wood

Insulating concrete forms (ICF) foundation

Dense packed cellulose insulation

High-efficiency windows

Geo-thermal HVAC

Heat recovery ventilator (HRV)

Recycled wood and reused timbers

Boot grate at front entry

No- and low-VOC paints, stains, and caulks

Low-flow toilets

Low-flow faucets and showerheads

ENERGY STAR appliances

Fluorescent lights

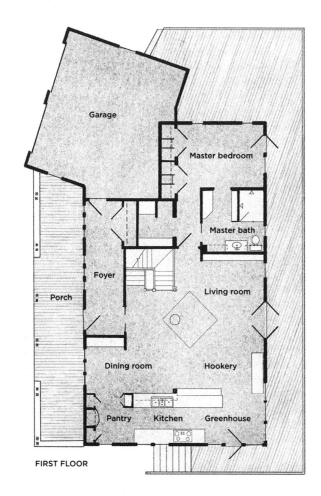

FIRST FLOOR

SECOND FLOOR

The shingle-style cottage design of the house reflects the houses of the Maine coast, which the couple love. The "car barn" was designed to align with the other two barns on the property.

Nobody would have blamed Kathy and David for being emotionally catatonic after a fire destroyed their two hundred-year-old house and everything in it. Yet the Vermont couple's immediate response was action.

As energetic professionals, the pair were accustomed to making decisions efficiently. Almost before the ashes had cooled, David was on the phone with 2morrow Studios and its principal architect and custom builder John Connell. Although he'd never designed or built with modular components before, Connell was familiar with the technology, which he recognized as the quickest strategy for replacing Kathy and David's home.

Making It Green

Old houses often exude wonderful character, but suffer from terribly inefficient energy systems. For their new home, Kathy and David decided to build a house that took its energy in tiny bites, enough to make it LEED certifiable. Constructing such a house would require substantial cooperation from a company called Customized Structure, Inc. (CSI), a modular manufacturer. John Connell usually selected and found the materials he needed without much trouble. But for this house, the manufacturer had to be on board with the stringent LEED requirements, which meant buying green materials from vendors that couldn't offer the customary volume discounts.

To make the house more energy efficient, John insisted CSI switch from their usual fiberglass insulation to cellulose insulation. He also asked them to use caulks and sealants free of VOCs, as well as certified wood. Although CSI normally used local wood (defined as being within a 500-mile radius), they had not maintained the necessary records to prove that the wood came from sustainably managed woodlots. Despite such setbacks, John succeeded in getting everything he needed for his clients' new home.

Their original farmhouse had been 3,500 square feet, bigger than these empty nesters needed. So Kathy and David opted for a more modest 1,800-square-foot home, which would be easier to heat, clean, and maintain. Unlike the drafty farmhouse that guzzled energy, the new house incorporated modern, energy-saving technologies such as a geothermal heating system, an insulated foundation, high-performance windows, and ENERGY STAR appliances and lighting. Sifting through the ashes of the original house, John managed to partially salvage some of the old timbers and some of the *ipe,* a sustainably harvested Brazilian decking material that they used for their kitchen floor.

Putting the Pieces Back Together

To relate it to the two barns that survived the fire, the new house was built on the same site as the original. John used an insulated concrete form (ICF) foundation because of its excellent energy efficiency, a critical consideration for the long Vermont winters. Gio Susini, 2Morrow's job captain, made sure the foundation walls were

The affordable kitchen cabinets were factory built, but made unique with an inlay of cherry bark onto each panel.

LEFT The latticework below has recently been planted with climbing hydrangeas and serves to connect the house with the landscape. The owners plan to plant grape vines on the upper trellis, an old Italian farm detail. The leaves will shade the house from the hot summer sun and bring texture and a look of antiquity.

ABOVE Delivered with the modules, the staircase was fitted together with the modules, though the handrail was produced and installed on site. The large French doors open to the deck, expanding the living space in the warmer months.

installed level, square, and plumb. A conventionally built house can usually be tweaked to fit onto a poorly aligned concrete foundation, but for the factory precision of a modular house, the foundation has to be equally meticulous.

On a snowy December day, six flatbed trailers arrived with the modules. Kathy and David watched with joy as their boxes were craned, one by one, snugly into place. As the last light of day faded, the final module was set in place. Just ten months later, Kathy and David moved into their new farmhouse. In the deep freeze of a Vermont winter, a typical site-built house would have taken much longer.

Modular construction provided a great advantage in building this house quickly. The modules arrived weather tight and allowed the crew to complete mechanical and interior work immediately, despite the weather. Exterior trim work was pre-installed, but John waited until the weather warmed to attach the cedar shingle siding. John introduced lots of texture to the house on-site with the cedar shingles, trellis, and latticework—and with the large overhangs that help protect the siding. He added many other engaging architectural details, such as the old New England "bulls-eye glass" transom windows above the kitchen door and the site-trimmed stairs.

According to John, factory fabrication is the key to providing custom homes at a more reasonable price. Although Kathy and David spent more than planned, the house ended up costing far less than LEED-certified, custom homes built the traditional way, slowly and on-site.

David and Kathy determined to emulate the early Americans who had built their original house—they created a home that fit their lifestyle and used the best technology available within their budget.

OPPOSITE A beautiful stone path runs between the 200-year-old horse barn and the new "car barn" to the outside deck which overlooks a lovely vista.

BELOW LEFT A section of the roof is lowered in to place.

BOTTOM LEFT AND RIGHT On a snowy day, the modules were set in place. (Photos by 2Morrow Studios LLC)

A sunspace off the kitchen allows a slow, sun-drenched breakfast and a view of the meadows. The red "bulls eye glass," an early hand-blown form of glass, is reminiscent of the owners' childhood cottage. The *ipe* wood floor, along with the beams, were salvaged from the original house. Not shown is Kathy's hookery, the area between this sunspace—or greenhouse, as Connell denotes it on the floor plan—where she does her hooked rugs.

The "bones" of the original house were reused to create the same timber-framed feel in the new one. A marble top and some site-built trim make this factory-built desk nook look custom.

Old News Is Good News

Cellulose insulation uses about 85 percent recycled newsprint, one of the largest waste contributors to landfills. Once it's been pulped and treated with boric acid to repel pests, wet cellulose can be sprayed into open walls or blown dry ("dense packed") into a closed wall behind either gypsum board or netting. Energy efficiency and cost increase along with density. In addition to reducing heat loss and air leaks, cellulose boasts a lower embodied energy, which means it takes less energy to produce this insulation than many other types. The installed cost of cellulose is often higher than fiberglass batt insulation because installers need training to install it. Nevertheless, it still represents a significantly less expensive insulation than any type of foam. For more information, to go www.cellulose.org.

ENERGY STAR Appliances

The U.S. Environmental Protection Agency and the U.S. Department of Energy's joint ENERGY STAR program rates energy-efficient appliances, which must exceed the federal minimum energy-efficiency standards for appliances by 15 to 20 percent. For example, ENERGY STAR dishwashers use less energy to heat the water than traditional models but also consume a gallon less water than hand washing. Refrigerators and freezers, which consume about 1/6 of all home electricity, cost about $125 per year to run for older models, compared to $100 or less for ENERGY STAR models. Most of a clothes washer's energy goes to heating water, and conventional machines use 25 to 40 gallons of water per cycle. These more efficient models use 10 to 50 percent less water and energy. For approximate operating costs and comparisons, look for EnergyGuide labels on all appliances. To learn more, visit www.energystar.gov.

The Mountain House

Modular

PHOTOGRAPHER:

Michael Rixon Photography

(unless otherwise noted)

ARCHITECT:

Ken Pieper

MANUFACTURER:

Epoch Homes

BUILDER:

Abode

LOCATION:

Plymouth, New Hampshire

SIZE:

1,680 square feet

RATINGS:

LEED-H—Platinum

NAHBGreen Certified—Gold

ENERGY STAR—5 Plus

Build Green NH—Gold certification

GREEN ASPECTS:

ICF Foundation

Passive solar

Cellulose in the ceiling

Spray foam insulation

Reclaimed oak flooring

No-VOC paints, carpets, and pads

Nontoxic caulks, sealers, and adhesives

Energy-efficient windows and doors

ENERGY STAR appliances and lighting

Composite decking

Dual-flush toilets

Low-flow showerheads

On-demand hot water heaters

Low-consumption drip irrigation system

Native landscaping

Drought-tolerant plants

Minimal lawn

Heat recovery ventilator

Timed bathroom and kitchen fans

ENERGY STAR ceiling fans

Materials with recycled content (e.g., sheetrock, countertops, etc.)

Low-VOC cabinetry

FSC-certified Wood

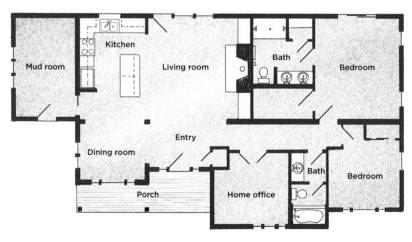

Floor Plan

BELOW The Mountain House was designed to function mainly as a vacation home for skiers. The natural cedar siding and green trim is typical of houses in the area.

OPPOSITE Icynene spray foam insulation was sprayed on and the excess was shaved off to create a very flat wall. Here a worker fills voids in the insulation. (Photo by Dave Wrocklage)

For years, Jack McBride and Bob Wildes built houses the way they first learned: on a vacant lot, one stick at a time.

Then things changed. When the old way suddenly no longer seemed the most effective, these two traditional home builders became interested in green building. To them, building green meant building houses that were more energy efficient, that kept the people inside healthy and comfortable, and that didn't waste materials.

Jack and Bob began to develop a prototype they called the Mountain House. Modular construction would limit waste and create a snug exterior tight and well-insulated enough to keep it warm through cold New Hampshire winters. The prototype was set in ski country, at the gateway to the White Mountains. The house would meld into the local ski communities but also adapt to suburbs.

Preaching Green

Jack and Bob decided that their house would meet the most stringent guidelines of the national green building certification programs. And as proof to the world, they would have the house certified green.

They chose the healthiest and most environmentally responsible building materials and systems available. And after creating the menu of design, construction, and system components for the house, they found that their Mountain House fit nicely on all the scales of green building.

However, at the open house, they discovered that "green" means different things to different people: no general understanding existed of what it meant to build a green house. Many of the homeowners they met at the open house knew almost nothing about green construction. But when they explained the energy efficiency of the house (which requires half the energy of a typical house to maintain and offers healthy indoor air and greater comfort), people started to take notice. They began to view the Mountain House with a new understanding.

Getting It Right

To give their house broader appeal, Jack and Bob designed it with higher than average ceilings: 11 feet in the foyer and living room. To accomplish this in a modular factory that is geared to build standard 8-foot ceilings took some effort, but the manufacturers designed a prefabricated truss and matching roof component that provided the height the builders wanted.

They found that factory construction offered other benefits as well. The framing of an ordinary house built on-site must be covered over quickly to protect it from the weather. Modular homes built inside a factory are kept out of the weather, so drywall can go on first, even before the outside walls are covered. That allows for a unique twist in energy-efficient construction.

Most houses—in or out of a factory—employ wood studs. On the inside, drywall is nailed to the stud; plywood is nailed to the other side of the stud on the outside. When nothing insu-

OPPOSITE Wainscoting, installed on-site, increases the traditional charm of this cozy den.

OPPOSITE A window high on the wall allows for ventilation and light to enter the room but provides privacy and room for furniture.

BELOW The master bedroom opens onto a small porch, diminishing the barrier between indoors and out.

NAHBGreen

The National Association of Home Builders (NAHB) first published *The Model Green Homebuilding Guidelines* in 2005 and in 2008 launched the NAHBGreen program to certify green homes and educate the building community and the general public about green building. The program aims to reduce environmental impact by providing guidance on a variety of building issues, including lot development, water and energy efficiency, building material resource efficiency, indoor environmental quality, and owner maintenance and operation. In 2009, NAHB published the *National Green Building Standard,* the only green building rating system to carry approval by the American National Standards Institute (ANSI). The NAHB-Green system is designed to be flexible enough to encourage geographically appropriate design and to be less cumbersome and therefore less costly than other programs. Homes seeking certification in the program must meet criteria in all categories of green construction (achieving either a Bronze, Silver, Gold, or Emerald score) and undergo at least two site inspections by an NAHBGreen Verifier. The program's "Green Approved" designation recognizes products that pre-qualify for points in the NAHBGreen program. Green Approved products include panelized walls, SIPs, or other forms of prefabricated building components including entirely modular construction. To learn more, visit www.nahbgreen.org.

No-Splinter Decks

A variety of composite decking products are on the market, most made from a mixture of plastic and wood, often which has been recycled. Along with their environmental benefits, the decking won't splinter or warp and requires minimal maintenance; best of all, it doesn't rot. A product that's recycled, that doesn't require paint, and that doesn't have to be replaced for years and years is about as green as it gets—and it saves you money as long as you own it. But the big bucks come up front: Composites generally cost up to three times as much as the price of wood. Many companies advertise that their products don't rot. To be sure, check that the material has been treated with a preservative such as zinc borate. To learn more, visit www.decks.com.

BELOW All kitchen appliances are ENERGY STAR rated. Cabinets were selected for their low VOC emissions.

BOTTOM The fireplace in the great room is a direct-vent closed system that doesn't use indoor air for combustion, which means no heat is lost. The fireplace warms the room with radiant heat.

The small porch on the front of the house serves as a comfortable place
to relax, but it also shades the living area from low hot summer sun.

lates the exterior wood from the wood stud
(wood is a poor insulating material), heat and
cold are quickly transmitted from inside to out
and vice versa.

Modular manufacturer Epoch Homes uses a
unique method of strapping (horizontal strips of
wood) across the interior walls, creating a space
between the wall stud and the sheetrock. When
the spray foam is applied, it totally fills the open
space between the studs and the space created
by the strapping. This results in a drastic reduction of thermal transmission and air movement
between the studs, creating an extremely energy
efficient wall system.

All the effort, planning, and thoughtful design
succeeded. The Mountain House was the first
house to be certified by NAHBGreen in New
Hampshire. Jack and Bob's project achieved
LEED and ENERGY STAR certifications as well.

EcoUrban House

Modular

PHOTOGRAPHER:

Susan Jackson

(unless otherwise noted)

ARCHITECT:

Garen Miller

MANUFACTURER:

Contempri Homes

BUILDER:

EcoUrban Homes

LOCATION:

St. Louis, Missouri

SIZE:

1,800 square feet

RATINGS:

LEED-H—Platinum

ENERGY STAR

GREEN ASPECTS:

Small footprint

Infill lot

Passive solar

ENERGY STAR appliances

High-efficiency hot water heater

Ballasted CFL lighting

Energy-efficient windows

Dual-flush toilets

Low-flow fixtures

Recycled floor tiles

No-VOC paints

Spray foam insulation

Bamboo floors

Composite decking

Fiber cement siding

Cool white rubber roof

Ceiling fans in high use areas

14 SEER high-efficiency heat pump

Native, drought-tolerant plants

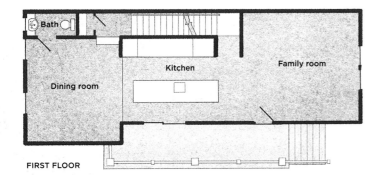

FIRST FLOOR

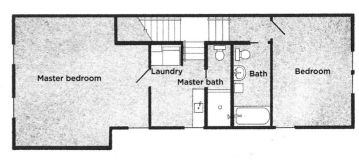

SECOND FLOOR

OPPOSITE Durable and low maintenance fiber cement siding is topped off by a TPO cool roof system, which reduces cooling costs and saves energy.

By nearly any measure, St. Louis is a city with problems.

Its crime rate is three times the national average. 25 percent of its population, including nearly 40 percent of its children, live in poverty. It's teen pregnancy rate is also double the national average. On top of that, large parts of the city's housing lies condemned and unfit for human habitation, interspersed with narrow, vacant lots.

Jay Swoboda knew he couldn't directly affect those other statistics, but the housing issue—that was something he could address. Jay, project manager for EcoUrban Homes, wanted to help rebuild St. Louis one narrow city lot at a time, filling discarded spaces with affordable, sustainable, attractive housing. Young professionals working in the city could also live in the city. Existing city residents would have better and more sustainable housing options.

Getting Started

EcoUrban's first project was in the Benton Park West neighborhood, two miles from downtown. Because they were willing to build on 30-foot-wide lots in depressed areas, the company got the property at a good price. For $6,000 they bought a narrow lot from a neighbor on the block, a cost far less than urban property elsewhere in St. Louis and in most large cities.

This type of urban renewal benefits the city and its middle-income residents, who can live close to parks, schools, restaurants, and work, reducing commuting costs and pollution and increasing opportunities in a community where property values rise as the desirability and ease of walking increase. This is the way St. Louis and most other American cities were before suburbs and interstates.

Beginning in college and continuing afterwards as a member of AmeriCorps and CORO, both volunteer community service organizations, Jay was concerned with affordable housing. In St. Louis, he recruited his college friend and fellow AmeriCorps alumni Nate Forst to join with him and Amos Harris, EcoUrban's president and owner, in an affordable housing startup. Together they called on architect Garen Miller to design a house that would be both affordable and attractive.

They decided to build their first house to LEED for Homes standards, to set an example in the city, even before the rating program's details were final. Pioneering LEED building brought challenges. The LEED specifications had not been finalized and no raters existed in the immediate area to review their project and assess its adherence to LEED goals. Despite all these issues, the EcoUrban House received the first LEED certification in Missouri, and became only the tenth in the country to achieve Platinum status, the highest LEED for Homes certification.

Building Modular

To build the house, Jay approached modular builder Contempri Homes.

Jay asserts that "modular construction is stronger and better insulated" than standard construction. It uses walls of 2 inches by 6 inches

LEFT Lifted by a crane, the first module is carefully set on the foundation. (Photo courtesy of EcoUrban)

BOTTOM Ready to be married to the first module, the second is set on the foundation. Because of the narrow lot, setting these modules was an unusual challenge for the manufacturer. (Photo courtesy of EcoUrban)

OVERLEAF All appliances are ENERGY STAR-rated. The compact fluorescent bulbs installed here use far less energy than incandescent bulbs and last for years. Thanks to a south-facing door and windows, natural light floods the kitchen, reducing the need for artificial light.

instead of the traditional 2 inch x 4 inch walls, providing an additional 2 inches of insulation, or an increase in R-value of 7.2. (The R-value is the ability of a material to resist the escape of heat.) "The factory is also very attentive to the amount of waste it incurs before delivering the product on-site, which translates to less waste in landfills," Jay says.

According to Nate, the biggest challenge remains educating people about prefab. Many people still associate modular houses with mobile homes. It takes a great deal of effort, and patience, to convince the public that modular construction can provide greater building speed, efficiency, and quality.

Contempri made adjustments to its standard construction methods to make the house LEED certifiable. They purchased special no-VOC paint and caulking for the house. They upgraded from double-hung windows to more efficient awning windows. Fluorescent bulbs replaced incandescents and spray-on Icycene foam insulation, which had normally been available only as an upgrade, went into the walls. Typical of modular construction, material waste was minimized, with cutoffs (or construction leftovers) from one project saved for others, rather than going into the dumpster, which is the norm in site-built construction.

The total construction waste for the house was about 1/4-pound per square foot compared to about four pounds per square foot for ordinary houses.

Conventional Green

Jay and Nate wanted their houses to be "conventional" green, to make them affordable for the local market. This first house would have no elaborate or innovative new systems, such as a photovoltaic or geothermal system. To stick to

a tight budget and keep the house affordable, they used traditional materials that would contribute to the energy efficiency of the house.

"We did everything we could in a conventional way to show that you could build a house without spending a great deal of money and still be able to be Platinum LEED certified," Jay said. Instead of spending money on expensive systems and finishes, they used all ENERGY STAR appliances, lighting, and windows, which cost only slightly more than many less efficient products. Low-maintenance and cost-effective fiber cement siding (see Fiber Cement Siding sidebar, opposite) went along the exterior walls. TPO (thermoplastic polyolefin) roofing, a cool roofing material, decreased the need for air conditioning and improved the cost efficiency (see Cool Roofs sidebar, opposite).

The spray-in Icynene insulation and high efficiency windows created a tight envelope that would conserve energy. The windows were positioned to take best advantage of solar gain in winter and to provide cross ventilation during warmer months. Daylighting was a consideration for the entire year in the placement of windows.

To conserve water, EcoUrban used dual-flush toilets, low-flow faucets, and installed native plants around the house that require little or no watering. With a high-efficiency heat pump, direct-vent hot water heating, and ceiling fans to move air, the house stays comfortable without costly technology. For the first year, utility bills—

gas, electric, water, and sewer—totaled $780, far below average for a typical house of its size.

The money left over in the budget was used to purchase sustainable materials such as bamboo flooring, which is a renewable resource, and recycled floor tiles for the bathrooms. Jay says he would have liked to use many more expensive finishes and modern technology, but he persisted in his goal to keep down costs to make the house practical and affordable for the local market.

Selling a New Idea

The house represented a new concept for urban St. Louis. Not only is it modular and green, but it sits in the inner city, an area that has seen more decline than growth in recent decades. When the house was complete, throngs of people attended an open house. Thanks to plenty of local publicity, more than a thousand people came through the house in the months after completion.

Nate believes that green building will not be fully successful until it is available to everyone. He hopes that high fuel costs and the growing interest of many young professionals in moving to urban areas close to work will produce in St. Louis and other faltering cities a growth of houses like the ones EcoUrban builds.

Both Jay and Nate live around the Benton Park West area where the first EcoUrban house was built. Both delight in their investment in their own neighborhood. Jay drives by the house nearly every day, proud of his company's first step towards the urban renewal of St. Louis.

OPPOSITE ABOVE Bamboo floors in the master bedroom and throughout the second floor come from the rapidly renewable plant, which can be harvested at maturity every five and-a-half to six years.

OPPOSITE BELOW An ENERGY STAR washer and dryer share space with the powder room on the second floor.

Fiber Cement Siding

Fiber cement siding consists of 90 percent cement/sand and 10 percent cellulose fiber and select additives mixed with water. It is available primed, stained, painted, or as raw siding in lap siding, panels, and shingles. A variety of textures are available, including smooth, or textured with a look of wood, stucco, stone, or brick. The siding is more durable than wood and works particularly well in hot, humid climates where siding is prone to rot and fungus. Because it doesn't have knots and other inconsistencies of wood, it is more durable and holds paint better, which reduces maintenance costs. In addition to its low maintenance, the siding resists moisture, cracking, fading, insect damage, fire, and impact damage. Most fiber cement products carry a thirty-to fifty-year warranty.

Cool Roofs

A cool roof reflects the sun's heat and radiation back into the atmosphere, so the roof surface stays cooler and reduces heat transfer into the living area below, keeping the house temperature down in warm weather. Many varieties of roofing material are highly reflective, including metal and TPO, or thermoplastic polyolefin, used here. The roofing doesn't have to be white to be cool, but can be treated with a reflective coating that allows dark colors to better deflect the sun's heat and radiation. Benefits include lower air conditioning use, lower utility costs, increased indoor comfort and less deterioration of roofing materials due to ultraviolet rays. To learn more, visit www.coolroofs.org.

Resource List

CONTEMPORARY FARMHOUSE

Architect
Christian Brown Design
11 Winding Brook Road
Jericho, VT 05465
802-899-1155
www.christianbrowndesign.com

Builder
Leach Construction of Vermont, LLC
30 Bradley Bow Road
Jericho, VT 05465
802-434-5578
www.leachconstructionvt.com

Interior Designer
Susan Fishman
Stowe Craft Design
55 Mountain Road
Stowe, VT 05672
802-253-7677
www.stowecraft.com

Photographer
Eric Roth Photography
www.ericrothphoto.com

Suppliers
Winterpanel (SIPs)
74 Glen Orne Drive
Brattleboro, VT 05301
802-254-3435
www.winterpanel.com

Arxx Building Products
(Insulated Concrete Forms)
www.arxxbuild.com

Pella Windows
www.pella.com

Kalwall Corp.
(shoji transluscent wall system)
www.kalwall.com

James Hardie (Fiber cement siding)
www.jameshardie.com

Englert Inc.
(standing seam metal roof)
www.englertinces.com

RenewAire (ERV)
www.renewaire.com

Environ Biocomposites LLC
(wheatboard kitchen cabinets and wall
panels)
www.environbiocomposites.com

Cheng Design Products (Concrete
kitchen countertops with color dyes
and additives)
www.concreteexchange.com

Teragren (bamboo flooring)
www.teragren.com

ECOsurfaces (rubber flooring)
www.ecosurfaces.com

3form (Ecoresin panels for kitchen
cabinet doors and office door)
www.3-form.com

Weyerhaeuser (TimberStrand LSL
[laminated strand lumber]
stair stringers and treads)
www.ilevel.com

NTI (direct-vent boiler)
www.nythermal.com

Myson Inc.
(hydronic panel radiators)
www.mysoninc.com

TUCKER BAYOU

Architect
J. Carson Looney, FAIA, Preston Bus-
sard, Chris Haley
Looney Ricks Kiss Architects, Inc.
175 Toyota Plaza
Suite 600
Memphis, TN 38103
901-521-1440
www.lrk.com

Modular Builder
Haven Custom Homes
1302 Concourse Drive
Suite 202
Linthicum, MD 21090
410-694-0091
www.havenhomes.com

On-site Builder
The St. Joe Company
WaterSound, FL

Interior Designer
Ann Nordeen Parker, ASID
Looney Ricks Kiss Architects, Inc.

Landscape Designer
Alan D. Holt, ASLA
Panama City Beach, Fl

Photographer
Jack Gardner
www.jackgardnerphoto.com

Suppliers
Sherwin-Williams (low-VOC paint)
www.sherwin-williams.com

HVAC–Lennox 16 SEER units
www.lennox.com

GE Profile appliances
www.geappliances.com

Rinnai
www.foreverhotwater.com

JELD-WEN windows
www.jeld-wen.com/windows/

James Hardie (fiber cement siding)
www.jameshardie.com

ARTIST STUDIO + RESIDENCE

Architect
Olle Lundberg
Lundberg Design
2620 Third Street
San Francisco, CA 94107
415-695-0110
www.lundbergdesign.com

Contractor
Malpas and Birmingham
962 Chula Vista Ave
Burlingame, CA 94010
415-760-0194 Bill Malpas
415-509-5799 Kevin Burmingham

Structural
Yu Strandberg Engineering
410 12th Street
Suite 200
Oakland, CA 94607
510-763-0475

Landscape Architect
Kikuchi & Associates
730 Mill Street
Half Moon Bay, CA 94019
650-726-7100

Suppliers
Metecno API (Metal Panels)
2000 Morgan Road
Modesto, CA 95358
800-377-5110

City Cabinetmakers
1351 Underwood Avenue
San Francisco, CA 94124
415-822-6161

Japan Woodworking and Design
233 So Maple Avenue #5
San Francisco, CA 94080

Westco Roofing
763 46th Avenue
Oakland, CA 94601

Brian Harris
Supreme Glass Company
(doors & windows)
1661 20th Street No. 4
Oakland, CA 94607
510-625-8995
www.supremeglass.net

Burris Window Shades
Rick Burris
323 14th Street
Oakland, CA 94612

TASC (Fire sprinklers)
1069 Sycamore Drive
Millbrae, CA 94030

THE BARN

Timberframe package
Bear Creek Timberwrights
1934 Middle Bear Creek Road
P.O. Box 335
Victor, MT 59875
406-642-6003
www.bearcreektimber.com

Builder
Rose & Bear home Builders, LLC
Big Sky Spur Road
Big Sky, Montana 59716
800-816-7734
www.roseandbear.com

Landscaping
Bear Paw Landscaping

Photographer
Roger Wade Studio
www.rogerwadestudio.com

Suppliers
Pozzi Windows
www.pozzi.com

Rocky Mountain Windows & Doors
(doors)
www.rockymountainwindows.com

Crestron Electronics Inc.
(automation system)
www.crestron.com

468 HOUSE

Architect
Jonathan Delcambre
www.jonathandelcambre.com
972-898-2841

Builder
Ferrier Custom Homes
11255 Camp Bowie West
Suite 115
Fort Worth, Texas 76008
817-237-6262
www.ferriercustomhomes.com

Landscape
Hocker Design Group
www.hockerdesign.com
214-915-0910

Suppliers
Blackson Brick
www.blacksonbrick.com

Design Within Reach
www.dwr.com

EnviroShield by Showcase (windows)
www.showcasewindows.com

Icynene (insulation)
www.icynene.com

Ikea (furnishings)
www.ikea.com

James Hardie (siding)
www.jameshardie.com

Premier Building Systems
www.pbssips.com

Rinnai (water heater)
www.foreverhotwater.com

A HOUSE OF STRAW

Architect
Brian Fuentes
Fuentes Design
1711 Pearl St. #201
Boulder, CO 80302
303-523-4654
www.fuentesdesign.com

Manufacturer & General Contractor
Jon Rovick Construction, Inc.
Dba Spirit Builders
P.O. Box 6927
Breckenridge, CO 80424
970-390-1561
www.jonrovick.com

Plastering
Anikke Storm
Stormworks
PO Box 849
Crestone, CO 81131
719-256-5215

Photographer
Roger Wade Studio
www.rogerwadestudio.com

Resources
Craftmade (fans)
www.craftmade.com

CHMI (sliding panel)
www.chmi.com

Valspar (blackboard paint)
88-313-5569

Authentic Pine Floors
www.authenticpinefloors.com

TALL + NARROW HOUSE

Designer/Builder
Randall Lanou
BuildSense Inc.
600 Foster St.
Durham, NC 27701-2109
919-667-0404
www.buildsense.com

Photographers
Charles Register—interiors
www.charlesregister.com

Eric Roth—exteriors
Eric Roth Photography
www.ericrothphoto.com

Suppliers
Anderson Windows & Doors
www.andersonwindows.com

Apex Cabinet Company
www.apexcabinet.com

Cement Board Fabricators
www.cbf11.com

Demilec (insulation)
www.demilecusa.com

Meld (countertops)
www.meldusa.com

Morningstar Bamboo Flooring
www.morningstarbamboo.com

Rinnnai (tankless water heater)
www.foreverhotwater.com

Superior Walls
www.superiorwalls.com

The Unico System (HVAC)
www.unicosystem.com

Union Corrugating Company
www.unioncorrugating.com

EASTBOURNE HOUSE

Architect
Boyd Montgomery
Watchorn Architect Inc.
416-385-1996
bmontgomery@wai-arch.com

Builder
Fifthshire
241 Applewood Cresent
Unit 3
Concord, Ontario, L4K 4E6
905-660-7415
www.fifthshire.com

Frame Manufacturer
Baily Metal Products
One Caldari Road
Concord, Ontario L4K 3Z9
800-668-2154
www.bmp-group.com

Interior Design
Tina Edwards
One Small Room
416-435-8660
tinaedwards@sympatico.ca

Photographer
Stacey Brandford Photography Inc.
Toronto, Canada
www.staceybrandford.com

Landscaper
Tom Madsen's Custom Interlocking &
Landscaping

Suppliers
Casa Bella Windows
www.casabellawindows.ca

VanEE (HRV)
www.vanee.ca

Heat N' Glo (fireplace)
www.heatnglo.com

Great Northern Insulation
(foam insulation)
www.gni.ca

Toto (low-flush toilets)
www.totousa.com

Home Corp. (water heater)
www.homeservices.com

THE PORRETTO HOUSE

Architect
Fred Pecceni
Pecceni Architecture
Mt. Pleasant, SC
www.peccini.com
843-849-7743

Builder
John Porretto
Sustainable Building Solutions
www.sbsbuilders.com
843-906-8780

Timber frame
Riverbend Timber Framing
www.riverbendtf.com
517-486-4355

Structural Insulated Panels
Insulspan
www.insulspan.com
800-726-3510

Photographer
Susan Sully
www.southerncosmopolitan.com
828-505-1908

Resources
Georgia Pacific (Dense Armor Plus)
www.gp.com

Isokern Fireplaces & Chimney Systems
www.isokern.net

Weru Windows & doors
www.weruwise.co.uk

WaterFurnace International, Inc.
www.waterfurnace.com

American Clay (natural plaster)
www.americanclay.com

Manibloc Plumbing System
www.viega-na.com
800-775-5039

THE PALMS HOUSE

Architect
Ron Radziner, Leo Marmol

Builder
Marmol Radziner Prefab
12210 Nebraska Avenue
Los Angeles, CA 90025
310-689-0089
www.marmolradzinerprefab.com

Photographer
David Lena Photography
3121 5th Street
Santa Monica, CA 90405
310-480-7007
www.davidlena.com

Suppliers
Bonded Logic Inc. (denim insulation)
www.bondedlogic.com

Caesarstone (countertops)
www.caesarstoneus.com

Carrier Corp. (HVAC System)
www.carrier.com

Dacor (appliances)
www.dacor.com

Eco Timber Flooring
www.ecotimber.com

Frigidaire (washer & dryer)
www.frigidaire.com

Hansgrohe (kitchen faucet)
www.hansgrohe-usa.com

Just Sinks
www.justsinks.com

Marmol Radziner Furniture
www.marmolradzinerfurniture.com

MechoShade (motorized solar shading)
www.mechoshade.com

Noritz (tankless water heater)
www.noritz.com

REBECCA LELAND FARMHOUSE

Manufacturer
Connor Homes
1741 Route 7 South
Middlebury, VT 05753
802-382-9082
www.connorbuilding.com

Builder
Columbia County Historic Homes
P.O. Box 218
North Chatham, NY 12132
518-766-7682

Photographer
Jim Westphalen
www.jimwestphalen.com

Photovoltaic Panel Contractor
Renewable Power Systems
Averill Park, NY
518-674-5808
www.rpspower.com

Hydronic solar Contractor
E2G
Peter Skinner
518-369-3208

Suppliers
Armstrong (linoleum flooring)
www.armstrong.com

Benjamin Moore (paints)
www.benjaminmoore.com

LifeBreath (ERV)
www.lifebreath.com

Muchkin (boiler)
www.munchkinboiler.net

StepCo (Cork flooring)
www.stepcofloors.com

THE METHOD CABIN

Architect
Balance Associates, Architects
80 Vine Street, Ste. 201
Seattle, WA 98121-1368
206-322-7737
www.balanceassociates.com

Builder & Manufacturer
Method Homes
2711 E. Madison Street, Ste. 211
Seattle, WA 98112
206.789.5553
www.methodhomes.net

Photographer
Lannie Boesiger
360-224-0353
www.lenzflarephotography.com

Suppliers
Bamboo Hardwoods Cabinets
www.bamboohardwoods.com

EcoTop Surfaces
www.kliptech.com

Timber Pro Coating (stains)
www.timberprocoatings.com

Sierra Pacific Windows
www.sierrapacificwindows.com

YOLO Colorhouse (no-VOC paints)
www.yolocolorhouse.com

Timber Pro UV (low-VOC stains)
www.timberprocoatings.com

Sierra Pacific Windows
www.sierrapacificwindows.com

Warmboard, Inc. (radiant floor panels)
www.warmboard.com

DIGS (furnishings)
www.digsshowroom.com

GE Appliances
www.geappliances.com

FARMHOUSE BUNGALOW

Designer
Peter Bergford
Scott Homes Inc.

Builder
Scott Homes Inc.
3016 10th Avenue NE
Olympia, WA 98506
360-357-9167
www.scotthomes.com

Manufacturer (SIPs)
Premier Panels
4609 70th Avenue East
Fife, WA 98424
800-275-708
www.pbssips.com

Suppliers
Rinnai
www.foreverhotwater.com

Sears (appliances)
www.sears.com

OSMO (stains and finishes)
www.ecowise.com (USA)
www.environmentalhomecenter.com (USA)
www.raincoastalternatives.com (Canada)

Milgard Windows
www.milgard.com

Windfall Lumber (reclaimed wood & FSC wood)
www.windfalllumber.com

THE WAVE COTTAGE

Designer
Pv+r, llc
P.O. Box 611161
Rosemary Beach, FL 32461
850-230-0777
www.pvandr.com

Manufacturer
Nationwide Custom Homes
1100 Rives Road
P.O. Box 5511
Martinsville VA 24115
800-216-7001
www.nationwidecustomhomes.com

Builder
Wave Construction
532 North Lakeshore Drive
Panama City Beach, FL 32413
850-249-2244

Interior Designer
Erika McPherson Powell
Urban Grace Interiors
205 West Mitchell Avenue
Santa Rosa Beach, FL 32459
850-231-9916
www.urbangraceinteriorsinc.com

Photographer
Jack Gardner Photography
www.jackgardnerphoto.com

Suppliers
Aprilaire (ventilation)
www.aprilaire.com

Cedar Valley (cedar shingle panel siding)
www.cedar-valley.com

CertainTeed (shingles)
www.certainteed.com

Hurd Windows and Doors
www.hurd.com

Jenn-Air (appliances)
www.jennair.com

Kohler (faucets)
www.kohler.com

Lovelace Designs (furnishings)
www.lovelaceinteriors.com

Sherwin Williams (no-VOC paint)
www.sherwin-williams.com

ECOFABULOUS HOUSE

Architect
Kanau Uyeyama
Architecton
2780 Alamein Ave.
Vancouver, BC V6L 1S2
Canada
604-736-1172
www.architecton.ca

Modular Manufacturer
Shelter Industries Inc.
3294–262nd St.
P.O. Box 1318
Aldergrive, BC V4W 2V1
Canada
800-561-3822
www.shelterindustries.com

Interior Design
Daine Halley
Comet Interior Design
604-939-1252
www.cometinteriordesign.com

Jan Rutgers
CMK Solutions
604-291-2033

Landscape Design
Houston Landscapes
328-309 West Cordova Street
Vancouver, BC
Canada
604-734-0907
www.houstonlandscapes.ca

Arcon Rock & Waterscapes
20074 92A Avenue
Langley, BC V1M 3A4
Canada
604-882-2027
www. Arconwaterdesigns.com

Photographers
Bob Matheson Photography
www.bobmathesonphotography.com

Martin Tessler
www.martintessler.com

Suppliers
All Weather Windows
www.allweatherwindows.com

CanHeat Hydronic Heating Products
(radiators)
604-538-8844

Cloverdale Paint
www.cloverdalepaint.com

Daltile (recycled tiles)
www.daltileproducts.com

Eveready Products Ltd.
(ventilation system)
www.evereadyproducts.com

Fire Busters
(sprinkler system)
www.firebusters.com

Interactive Living
(home control system)
www.interactiveliving.ca

Miles Fireplace
www.milesfireplaces.com

SLS-Light Source
www.sls-lighting.com

Solus Décor
(Concrete tiles for fireplace & entry)
www.solusdecor.com

Toto Toilet
www.wolseleyinc.ca

Trout Creek Enterprises
(wood siding & decking)
www.troutcreekenterprises.com

Viessmann Manufacturing Co. Ltd
(heating system)
www.viessmann.ca

GLEN CAIRN COTTAGE

Manufacturer
Nationwide Custom Homes
1100 Rives Road
P.O. Box 5511
Martinsville, VA 24115
800-216-7001
www.nationwide-homes.com

Designer & Developer
Carl Krave
Pocket Neighborhoods, Inc.
410 Beltrees Street
Dunedin, FL 34698
727-734-1229
www.glencairncottages.com

Landscape Architect
Drew Copley
Copley Design Associates, Inc.
1666 Laney Drive
Palm Harbor, FL 34683

Interior Designer
Denise Beamer
Designer's Difference
727-734-7293
www.designersdifference.com

Green Certification Consultant
Rich Badders
Shoreline Design Group
793 San Christopher Dr.
Dunedin, FL 34698
727-736-5463
www.shorelinesdesigngroup.com

Photographer
Jim Goins Photography
www.jimgoinsphotography.com

Suppliers
Lennox (HVAC)
www.lennox.com

Rinnai (tankless water heater)
www.rinnai.us

Shwinco (hurricane impact windows)
www.shwinco.com

Raynor (garage doors)
www.raynor.com

Jeld-Wen (doors)
www.jeld-wen.com

LP Corporation (Radiant barrier)
www.lpcorp.com

HEATHER'S HOME

Builder
Ferrier Builders
11255 Camp Bowie West #115
Ft. Worth, TX 76008
817-237-6262
www.ferriercustomhomes.com

Architect
Gary Gene Olp
GGOArchitects
5646 Milton
Dallas, TX 75206
214-328-9091
www.ggoarchitects.com

SIP Erection & Framing
TR Framing
214-460-0042

Photographer
Terry Granger Photography
terri@glanger.com

Suppliers
Acme Bricks (glass blocks)
www.acmebrick.com

Cooper Lighting (light fixtures)
www.cooperlighting.com

FisherSIPs (SIPs panels)
www.fishersips.com

Daikin Heating & Cooling
www.daikin.com

Delta Faucets
www.dealtafaucet.com

Feeney (wire stair rail)
www.feeneywire.com

Howard Garrett (landscape plan)
Dirt Doctor
www.dirtdoctor.com

James Hardie Siding
www.jameshardie.com

Jeld-Wen (windows)
www.jeldwen.com

Rainfilters
www.rainfilters.com

Renovation by Design (cabinets)
www.rbdgeneral.com

Sherwin-Williams
www.sherwin-wlliams,com

Solar Systems Installations
www.solarsysinstall.com

Therma-Tru (doors)
www.thermatru.com

Toto USA, Inc. (toilets & sinks)
www.totousa.com

THE MKLOTUS

Architect
Michelle Kaufmann Designs
www.mkd-arc.com

Manufacturer
XtremeHomes
4801 Feather River Blvd #17
Oroville CA 95965-9692
530-230-4933
www.xhllc.com

Landscape Architect
Late Afternoon Garden Design
310 North School St.
Ukiah, CA 95482
707-462-5133
www.lateafternoon.com

Photographer
John Swain Photography

Suppliers
Mitsubishi Electric (solar panels)
www.mitubishielectric.com

NanaWall (folding door system)
www.nanawall.com

Bedrock Industries (recycled glass tile)
www.bedrockindustries.com

Velux America Inc. (skylight)
www.velux.com

Progress Lighting
www.progresslighting.com

Sierra Pacific Windows
www.sierrapacificwindows.com

Kohler (fixtures & fittings)
www.kohler.com

DalTile (ceramic tile)
www.daltile.com

3Form (sliding door panels)
www.3-form.com

Cembonit (siding)
www.cbf11.com

Yolo Colorhouse (paint)
www.yolocolorhouse.com

Berg & Berg (flooring)
www.beronio.com

Concreteworks (countertops & island)
www.concreteworks.com

Whirlpool (appliances)
www.whirlpool.com

Marin Outdoor Living (fireplace)
www.marinoutdoorliving.com

KitchenAid (stovetop)
www.kitchaid.com

Home Director
www.homedirector.com

Rana Creek (living roof)
www.ranacreek.com

POWERHOUSE

Architect
John D. Rossi
The Barendsen Rossi Collaborative
Newburyport, MA
www.brcollaborative.com

Modular Manufacturer
Epoch Homes
107 Route 106
Pembroke NH 03275
877-463-7624
www.epochhomes.com

Builder
NJZ Developers LLC
22 Bel Air Road
Hingham, MA
781-740-1388

Development Company
PowerHouse Enterprises, Inc.
60 Island Street
Lawrence, MA 01840
www.powerhouse-enterprises.com

Landscaper
Ould Towne Gardens
978-499-0038

Photographer
Eric Roth Photographer
www.ericrothphoto.com
978-887-1975

Resources
Hampton Bay (ceiling fans)
www.hamptonbay.com

Circle Furniture (furniture)
www.circlefurniture.com

Frigidare (appliances)
www.frigidaire.com

Sterling A Kohler Co.(toilets & faucets)
www.sterlingplumbing.com

Icynene (insulation)
www.icynene.com

Old Castle Pre-cast (foundation)
www.oldcastleprecast.com

Pella (windows)
www.pella.com

LP SmartSide (siding)
www.lpcorp.com

Home slicker Plus (rainscreen)
www.benjaminobdyke.com

Advantech (sheathing)
www.huberwood.com

Benjamin Moore–Aura line (paints)
www.benjaminmoore.com

Renmar (ERV)
www.renmar.ca

Solar Wave (monitoring system)
www.solarwave.com

LEAFHOUSE

Builder
University of Maryland
College Park, Maryland

Photographer
Jim Tetro Photography
703-876-0686
www.jimtetro.com

Faculty Advisor
Amy E. Gardner
University of Maryland

Resources
SANYO Energy (USA) Corporation
(PV solar panels)
www.us.sanyo.com

UltimateAir (ERV)
www.ultimateair.com

Lutron (lighting control system)
www.lutron.com

Apricus (solar hot water system)
www.apricus.com

Steibel Eltron (tankless water heater)
www.stiebel.com.au

Ecotimber (tigerwood flooring)
www.ecotimber.com

Luke Works, Inc (concrete countertop)
www.lukeworks.com

Panelite (laminated panels)
www.e-panelite.com

Tradewood Doors & Windows
www.tradewoodindustries.com

Warmboard Radiant Subfloor, Inc.
www.warmboard.com

ATAS International, Inc. (metal siding)
www.atas.com

BioBased Insulation (Soy based
insulation)
www.biobased.net

Benjamin Obdyke (rainscreen house-
wrap)
www.benjaminobdyke.com

Creative Laundry
www.creativelaundry.com

Eon (recyclable decking)
www.eonoutdoor.com

Emory Knoll Farms, Inc. (green roof
plants)
www.greenroofplants.com

Heyes Forest Products Inc. (Eastern
White Pine siding)
www.heyesforest.com

Jennifer Gilmer Kitchen & Bath (bamboo kitchen cabinets by Corsi)
www.jennifergilmerkitchens.com

Kohler
www.kohler.com

LEDFolio (LED fixtures)
www.ledfolio.com

North Creek Nurseries, Inc.
(Native plants)
www.northcreeknurseries.com

HIGHLAND HOUSE

Architect
Brad Tomecek
Studio H:T
1445 Pearl Street
Suite 208
Boulder, Colorado 80302
303-247-0405
www.studioht.com

Manufacturer
Barvista Homes
390 Mountain View Road
Berthoud, Colorado
970-532-4257
www.barvistahomes.com

Builder
John Cianci
Eco-Infill

Landscape Architect
Paul Turnburke
Turnburke & Associates

Lighting Consultant
Emily Koonce
Element Lighting

Energy Consultant
Megan Gilman
Active Energies

Photographer
Ben Tremper
www.bentremper.com

Resources
Carlisle (recycled rubber paver tiles)
www.carlisle-syntec.com

Danze (plumbing fixtures)
www.danze.com

Heatilator (gas fireplace)
www.heatilator.com

Kwal (low-VOC paint)
www.kwalpaint.com

Kohler (sinks)
www.kohler.com

LIVING HOME

Architect
Ray Kappe
Kappe + Du Architects
310-459-7791
www.kappedu.com

Builder
Living Homes
2910 Lincoln Blvd.
Santa Monica, CA 90405
310-581-8500
www.livinghomes.net

Interior Designer
Heidi Toll Design
www.heiditolldesign.com
818-906-2444

Garden Designer
Richard Grigsby
The Great Outdoors Landscape Design
& Construction
21448 Entrada Rd.
Topanga, CA 90290
310-455-0348
www.greatoutdoorlandscapedesigns.
com

Photographer
CJ Berg/Sunshine Divis
Tom Bonner

Resources
Permacity/Gridpoint
(photovoltaic system)

ACME Environmental and Creative
Climate (radiant floors)
www.acmegreen.com

Bonded Logic Inc. (denim insulation)
www.bondedlogic.com

Bosch (appliances)
www.boschappliances.com

Permalight (LED lights)
www.americanpermalight.com

Panasonic (fans)
www.panasonic.com

Tamarack Technologies, Inc.
(whole-house fan)
www.tamtech.com

AFM Safecoat (paints & stains)
www.afmsafecoat.com

Paperstone (countertops)
www.paperstoneproducts.com

Oceanside Glasstile
(recycled glass tiles)
www.glasstile.com

Coverings Etc.
(recycled porcelain tiles)
www.coveringsetc.com

Matteo (bedding)
www.mateohome.com

Kohler (fixtures)
www.kohler.com

EnviroGLAS Products Inc.
(recycled glass countertops)
www.enviroglasproducts.com

Carlisle–Syntec (roofing)
www.carlisle-syntec.com

Jacuzzi
www.jacuzzi.com

Fleetwood Windows & Doors
www.fleetwoodusa.com

The Reuse People
www.thereusepeople.org

Design Within Reach (furniture)
www.dwr.com

PolyGal (window panels)
www.polygal.com

BACK FROM THE BURN

Architect/Builder
John Connell
2Morrow Studio
P.O. Box 313 Warren VT 05674
802-496-5546
www.2morrowstudio.com

Photographer
Carolyn L. Bates Photography
PO Box 1205
Burlington, Vermont 05402
802-862-5386
www.carolynbates.com

Resources
Eco-Block (ICF)
www.eco-block.com

Pella Windows & doors
www.pella.com

WaterFurnace (geothermal system)
www.waerfurnace.com

American Aldes Ventilation Corp.
(HRV)
www.americanaldes.com

Sherwin-Williams (paint)
www.sherwin-williams.com

Cabot (low-VOC stain)
www.cabostain.com

Toto USA
www.totousa.com

Kenmore (ENERGY STAR refrigerator)
www.sears.com

Frigidaire (ENERGY STAR dishwasher)
www.frigidaire.com

THE MOUNTAIN HOUSE

Manufacturer
Epoch Homes
107 Route 106
Pembroke NH 03275
877-463-7624
www.epochhomes.com

Builder
Abode
9 Trafalgar Square, Suite 120
Nashua, NH 03063
603-882-2333
www.YourAbodeHome.com

Architect
Ken Pieper
www.stonemountaincabins.com

Interior Designer
Design East Interiors
www.designeastinteriors.com

Landscape Architect
Douglas Weeman
Andrews Construction

Photographer
Michael Rixon Photography
1 Meadow Lane
Bow, NH
603-228-2362
www.rixonphotography.com

Suppliers
Icynene (insulation)
www.icynene.com

Logix (ICF foundation)
www.logixicf.com

Trex decking (Brasilia Cayenne
decking)
www.trex.com

Carlisle (reclaimed oak flooring)
www.carlislewideplankfloors.com

Crown Point Cabinetry
www.crown-point.com

IceStone (countertop in guest bath)
www.icestone.biz

IKO (30-yr architectural roofing
shingles)
www.iko.com

Wolf range
www.wolfrange.com

Asko (dishwasher)
www.askousa.com

SubZero (refrigerator)
www.subzero.com

Pella (windows)
www.pella.com

Rheem (high-Efficiency gas furnace)
www.rheem.com

Seagull Ceiling Fans
www.seagulllighting.com

ECOURBAN HOUSE

Architect
Garen Miller
5115 St. Charles Place
St. Charles, MO 64119
314-645-1777
www.garenmiller.com

Developer
EcoUrban Homes
906 Olive Street
Suite 1212
St. Louis, MO 63101
314-231-0400
www.ecourbanhomes.com

Modular Manufacturer
Contempri Industries, Inc.
P.O. Box 69
Pinckneyville, illinois 62274-0069
618-357-5361
www.contemprihomes.com

Photographer
Susan Jackson
www.susanjacksonphoto.com

Resources
Anderson (windows)
www.andersonwindows.com

James Hardie (fiber cement siding)
www.jameshardie.com

Humabuilt (interior doors)
www.humabuilt.com

Natural Cork (bamboo floors)
www.naturalcork.com

Poliform USA (kitchen cabinets)
www.varenna.com

Sherwin Williams (paint)
www.sherwin-williams.com

Trex (composite decking)
www.trex.com

Editor: Rebecca Kaplan
Designer: Darilyn Lowe Carnes
Production Manager: Jules Thomson

Library of Congress Cataloging-in-Publication Data:

Koones, Sheri, 1949-
  Prefabulous and sustainable: building and customizing an affordable,
energy-efficient home / Sheri Koones; foreword by Robert Redford.
      p. cm.
  ISBN 978-0-8109-8483-7 (hardcover)
1. Prefabricated houses. 2. Sustainable architecture. 3. Architecture,
Domestic. I. Title.
  NA7145.K66 2010
  728'.0472—dc22

                        2009032546

Abrams books are available at special discounts when purchased
in quantity for premiums and promotions as well as fundraising
or educational use. Special editions can also be created to
specification. For details, contact specialmarkets@abramsbooks.com
or the address below.

ABRAMS
THE ART OF BOOKS SINCE 1949
115 West 18th Street
New York, NY 10011
www.abramsbooks.com

PAGE 2 The home's two modules connect at the entranceway. Bright colors
add a touch of surprise and are an inexpensive way of adding design elements.
(Photo by Martin Tessler)

PAGE 6-7 The Rebecca Leland Farmhouse is located in Chatham, New York,
and fits in with the many historic houses in the area.